Long Gone

DARYL CUMBER DANCE

Long Gone

*The Mecklenburg Six
and the Theme of Escape
in Black Folklore*

The University of Tennessee Press

KNOXVILLE

Frontispiece: Fences and guard tower at Mecklenburg Correctional
Center. Grateful acknowledgment is made to Richmond Newspapers,
Inc., for permission to use this photograph.

The paper used in this book meets the minimum requirements of the
American National Standard for Permanence of Paper for Printed
Library Materials, z39.48-1984. Binding materials have been chosen for
durability. ∞

Library of Congress Cataloging-in-Publication Data

Dance, Daryl Cumber.
    Long gone.

    Bibliography: p.
    Includes index.
1. Mecklenburg Six (Group) 2. Prisoners—Virginia—
Biography. 3. Fugitives from justice—Virginia—
Biography. 4. Escape—Virginia—Case studies.
5. Afro-Americans—Folklore. 6. Mecklenburg Correctional
Center (Va.) I. Title.
HV8657.D36   1987   365'.641   86-7097
ISBN 0-87049-512-7 (alk. paper)

Contents

Illustrations

Acknowledgments

Grateful acknowledgment is made to Richmond Newspapers, Inc., Richmond, Virginia, for permission to use the photographs of Derick Peterson and Earl Clanton, Willie Leroy Jones, Lem Tuggle, James Briley, and Linwood Briley and for permission to reproduce three cartoons by Gary Brookins and two by Bob Gorrell; to Ben R. Johns, Jr., AIA, Architect, and the Virginia Department of Corrections for permission to reproduce Ben R. John's drawing of the Mecklenburg Correctional Center; to Liveright Publishing Corporation for permission to reprint "Runagate Runagate" from *Angle of Ascent: New and Selected Poems by Robert Hayden,* copyright © 1975, 1972, 1970, 1966 by Robert Hayden; to Maurice Duke for the photograph of the author; and to Kimberly Pugh for the drawing of James Briley.

A project of this type required the cooperation, assistance, advice, and contributions of such a vast number of people that it is impossible to thank each individually for his or her specific contribution; indeed I do not even know the names of many of those who assisted me in various significant ways.

First of all I want to recognize a few of the many faithful family and friends who have helped me keep my sanity through the preparation of five books, who have always been there for me, encouraging and supporting me and promoting my work. Thank you Warren C. Dance, Sr., Veronica B. Cumber, Daryl Lynn Dance, Randy and Wendy Johnson, Ronald and Clara Lewis, Elaine Crocker, Frankie O'Mealy, Charlene Warner, Carolyn Blount, and Florence Cooper.

In recognizing those who have contributed directly to the preparation of this project, I wish to express my deep gratitude to Carol Orr of the University of Tennessee Press for her encourx agement and support of this project. I am also grateful to Roger Abrahams and Trudier Harris for their helpful responses to my proposal for the study; and to Trudier Harris, Philip J. Schwarz, Napoleon Peoples, Dorothy Scura, and Warren Dance, Jr., for their perceptive and sensitive readings of the final draft of this manuscript. Corrections and suggestions offered by all of these readers have been gratefully incorporated into this work.

Much of the information about the escape and many of the responses to it came from inmates in Virginia penitentiaries. Two of the men whose invaluable contributions over a long period of time deserve special recognition are Larry Batten and Charles Satchell. Among others who contributed in various ways are A. Bellizer, David X. Brown, Wilbert L. Evans, Evans D. Hopkins, Calvin Hudson, Jamal, Emmett O. Johnson, Joseph Jones, Frank Lee, Derick Lynn Peterson, "Monster" Rainey, Reverend Jerome L. Russ, Harry D. Seigler, Michael Smith, Tracy X, Lem Tuggle, Willie Lloyd Turner, W. Winfrey, and A. Woodfin.

Many of the officials in the Virginia Department of Corrections granted interviews, provided information and advice, or assisted me in various other ways; among these people are Robert M. Landon, former director, Allyn R. Sielaff, former deputy secretary of Public Safety and former director of the Department of Corrections, Lonnie L. Thomas, administrative assistant, and Jim Jones, administrative assistant; and on the staff of the Virginia State Penitentiary, Kathi King, operations officer, Jim Christianson, program director, James Jackson, counselor, and Reverend Odie Brown, chaplain; and Edward Pickett, assistant coordinator of Chapter I Programs, Rehabilation School Authority. I am grateful also to the guards and other personnel of the Mecklenburg Correctional Center who assisted me but whom I consider it judicious to leave anonymous.

I also wish to thank Virginia Lieutenant Governor L. Douglas Wilder and Carolyn Moss, secretary of administration, State of Virginia, for their advice and encouragement during this project.

Among the law officials who were in varying ways involved with the subjects of this study and who discussed them with me and/or provided me information, I wish to thank Sgt. Norman

Harding, supervisor of Sex Crimes and Homicide Investigations, Richmond Police Department; FBI agents Jim Trotter, Steve Drewes, and Michael Carbonell; and Randy Boyd, the Charles City commonwealth attorney.

I want to thank WXEX TV, Channel 8, Richmond, for allowing me to visit and record their video tape of the James Briley press conference; and Philip J. Schwarz for making available to me his research and studies on slaves and crime in Virginia and for leading me to other useful sources. For additional information, advice, and assistance I also wish to acknowledge Paul W. Keve, Joe and JoAnn Pugh, Jean Ferguson, Robert Terry, Jr., Herman Carter, Sue James, LaVerne Spurlock, and Annie Williams.

I am grateful to those members of the office staff of the English department at Virginia Commonwealth University who took the telephone messages and photocopied and offered varied clerical assistance, especially Norma Middleton, Sharon Call, and Greg Jenkins. I am also indebted to my son Allen C. Dance for technical assistance in the preparation of this manuscript.

Grateful acknowledgment is due a number of people whose names I do not have: the many guards who were both gracious and professional in receiving me and providing me escort when I visited the prisons; the many librarians at numerous area libraries, especially at the Richmond Newspapers Library, who provided me assistance in my research; the numerous secretaries, receptionists, and clerks who took messages, made appointments, located information, copied materials, and/or provided directions at the Department of Corrections; the office of the secretary of Transportation and Public Safety, State of Virginia; the Virginia State Penitentiary; the Charles City Court House; the Richmond Circuit Criminal Court; the Henrico Circuit Criminal Court; the Virginia State Police Headquarters; the offices of the FBI in Richmond, Virginia, Philadelphia, Pennsylvania, and Charlotte, North Carolina; the Richmond Police Headquarters; the Richmond Public Schools; the Richmond newspapers, various radio and television stations, and numerous other agencies.

I am grateful also to the many other citizens who talked with me but who chose to remain anonymous.

Acknowledgments

These warm acknowledgments are not intended to conceal the fact that some individuals, including personnel at some of the above-cited institutions, were not cooperative, were consistently unavailable, failed to provide materials they frequently promised, and in other ways created obstacles and caused me a great deal of frustration, lost time, and wasted energy. I trust that they know who they are and will not presume any of the accolades are intended for them.

Frequently Cited Works

American Negro Folklore. J. Mason Brewer. *American Negro Folklore.* Chicago: Quadrangle, 1968.

American Negro Folksongs. Newman White. *American Negro Folksongs.* 1928; rpt. Hatboro, Penn.: Folklore Associates, 1965.

Blues Fell This Morning. Paul Oliver. *Blues Fell This Morning: The Meaning of the Blues.* New York: Horizon Press, 1960.

Commonwealth Times. Virginia Commonwealth University, *Commonwealth Times.*

Deep Down. Roger D. Abrahams. *Deep Down in the Jungle: Negro Narrative Folklore from the Streets of Philadelphia.* 1st rev. ed. Chicago: Aldine, 1970.

Encyclopedia of Black Folklore. Henry D. Spalding, ed. *Encyclopedia of Black Folklore and Humor.* Middle Village, New York: Jonathan David, 1972.

Fysk. Fysk Magazine. (An inmate publication printed at the Virginia State Penitentiary in Richmond.)

Get Your Ass in the Water. Bruce Jackson. *"Get Your Ass in the Water and Swim Like Me": Narrative Poetry from Black Oral Tradition.* Cambridge: Harvard Univ. Press, 1974.

The Life. Dennis Wepman, et al. *The Life: The Lore and Folk Poetry of the Black Hustler.* Philadelphia: Univ. of Pennsylvania Press, 1976.

Negro Spirituals. Christa K. Dixon. *Negro Spirituals: From Bible to Folk Song.* Philadelphia: Fortress Press, 1976.

Negro Tales from Pine Bluff. Richard M. Dorson, *Negro Tales from Pine Bluff, Arkansas, and Calvin, Michigan.* Bloomington: Indiana Univ. Press, 1970.

Negro Workaday Songs. Howard W. Odum and Guy B. Johnson. Negro Workaday Songs. 1916; rpt. New York: Negro Universities Press, 1926.

NL. The Richmond News Leader.

Long Gone

Prologue

On May 31, 1984, six condemned men (Linwood Briley, James Briley, Earl Clanton, Jr., Willie Leroy Jones, Derick Lynn Peterson, and Lem Tuggle) incarcerated in the Mecklenburg Correctional Center in Boydton, Virginia, engineered the biggest, the most daring, the most ingenious, and the most spectacular Death Row escape ever attempted. In a brash and bold move they, with the help of some fellow inmates, took absolute control of the Death Row area, posed as prison guards, ordered a van, directed that the gates be opened, and drove away from the penitentiary, issuing one final command, "Close the gates!" Their astonishing escape was accomplished without any violent confrontations or injuries. The guards were caught so off guard and lured and entrapped so cunningly that they had no opportunity to offer any effective resistance. Indeed the feat was effected with such finesse that one escapee, Linwood Briley, would later insist, "We didn't *break* out of prison. . . . We walked out" (quoted by Reverend Odie Brown, interview, Richmond, Virginia, June 17, 1985). Even the escapees were incredulous at the success of their act: escapee Lem Tuggle asserted, "We couldn't believe that they had actually let us out like that" (conversation, Richmond, June 28, 1985).

The magnitude of the escape, the sheer audacity of it, and the notoriety of the escapees, particularly the infamous Briley brothers, coupled with the terror it inspired throughout the state of Virginia, up and down the East Coast, and even into Canada, evoked memories of the numerous exploits of fugitives and outlaws on the run in Black folktales, Black toasts, Black music, and Black literature. The participants, the escape (frequently dubbed "The Great Escape"), the search, the capture, daily recorded in papers and TV news stories, constantly recalled to mind characters and echoes and lines and themes from numerous such accounts. At the same time that traditional, recorded lore prophesied and foreshadowed and echoed each unfolding scene in the drama, contemporary bards recorded and responded to this spectacular coup with familiar new poems and tales and toasts. The response of the folk made it quite clear that not only was the escape replaying the oldest and most enduring theme in Black folklore and literature, but it was also introducing fascinating new, but at the same time familiar, variations on that theme.

As the six desperate men drove out of Mecklenburg's famed maximum security unit at 10:47 P.M. on May 31, 1984, and headed toward North Carolina, they were also entering history and legend—whether they knew it or not—and bards were already poised to begin to record and immortalize their exploits (as well as to satirize and lampoon their blunders).

> Late one night in the heat of May
> Six brave comrades made their getaway.
>
> Joseph Jones, Virginia State Penitentiary
> August 6, 1984

Long Gone

Long Gone

CHAPTER 1

"He's Long Gone"

The Theme of Escape in Black Folklore and Literature

Leader: It's a Long John.
Group: Long John.
Leader: He's long gone.
Group: Long gone.
Leader: Like a turkey through the corn.
Group: Like a turkey through the corn.
Leader: He's long gone.
Group: Long gone.

> Traditional worksong celebrating Long John's outrunning
> the sheriff and the deputies and their bloodhounds
> in his flight from the chain gang to freedom.

Throughout their experiences in this country, certain segments of the Black population have viewed themselves as enslaved, whether they were chattel owned by slaveowners prior to emancipation, whether they were impressed into peonage and forced to work on white plantations and in chain gangs after slavery, whether they were victims of sharecropping systems that virtually reenslaved them during the twentieth century, whether they were the repressed and disfranchised and persecuted in Southern Jim Crow towns throughout the first half of the twentieth century, whether they are those trapped by unemployment and poverty today, or whether they are among the Blacks who continue to be disproportionately represented in our penal institutions. One has only to talk to contemporary Black slum dwellers, Black prison inmates, and a host of other Blacks as well who may not be ensnared in those situations to have reinforced the observation made by William H. Grier and Price M. Cobbs, "For white America to understand the life of the black man, it must recognize that so much time has passed and so little has changed."[1]

For any individual who is enslaved, incarcerated, constrained, the major goal is freedom. Escape from his or her present entrapment has been the major theme in the Black American's folklore and literature from its beginnings. Slave songs are full of images of escape, some clearly escape from slavery, others apparently escape from this world—which becomes a safe metaphor for expressing the compelling desire for an escape from bondage. The slave sang, "No more hundred lash for me, / No more driver's lash for me, / Many thousand gone." He intoned, "Swing low, sweet chariot, coming for to carry me home." He advised, "Steal away, steal away, steal away to Jesus." He acclaimed, "The gospel train is coming . . . Get on board, children, get on board." He extolled, "Oh, freedom. Oh, freedom. Oh freedom over me, and before I'll be a slave, I'd be buried in my grave and go home to my Lord and be free." He appealed, "Go down, Moses, / Way down in Egypt land, / Tell old Pharoah, / Let my people go / . . . . O, let us all from bondage flee." He taunted, "The devil he thought he had me fast. . . . But I thought I'd break his chains at last." He acclaimed, "I am bound for the land of Canaan." Slave and later tales recount escapes from Ole Master, the paterollers, sheriffs, posses, Ku-Kluxers, bigger and stronger animals, ghosts, the devil, the Lord, or prison. In "Convict's Prayer," the speaker, paraphrasing the twenty-third Psalm, concludes, "Surely goodness and mercy shall find me one of these days in my life / and I will drill away from this house for ever and ever" (*Get Your Ass in the Water*, p. 216). Many is the tale that ends in lines similar to these from *S&J*: "I was makin' *feet* help the *body*! Yes, Lawd, I was gettin' out the way" (p. 32).

Lacking the political, economic, and military might to win freedom through legal means, through the attainment of economic power, or through revolution,[2] the Black people in this country have found that their best chance for freedom was through running—literally and figuratively. In the Black folk lexicon, noted for its flexibility, its originality, and its vivid metaphors, there is no idea that has so many different words to express it as the idea of leaving, fleeing, running.[3] There is no trait that is regarded as more critical to survival than the ability to run; there is no characteristic more applauded than skill at running:

> You see, the raccoon, you know, he was an engineer
> And the possum, he always tend to the switch,
> Old rabbit didn't have no job at all
> But he was a running son-of-a-bitch.[4]
>
> *Negro Tales from Pine Bluff*, p. 24

> [Dis nigger] jumped de fence and run fru de paster,
> White man run, but nigger run faster.
> . . . .
> Dat nigger run, dat nigger flew,
> Dat nigger tore his shirt in two.
>
> *Encyclopedia of Black Folklore*, p. 239

> Take dis ole hammer an' carry it
>   to the cap'n
> And tell him I'm gone.
>
> If he ask you was I runnin', tell him
>   no, I was might' near flyin'.
>
> *American Negro Folklore*, p. 195

Countless tales and songs in the folk tradition have lines that encourage, "Run, nigger, run, or the paterollers will catch you"; "O, run, nigger, run, cause it's almos' day"; or acclaim, "You ought to see that preacher [nigger, man] run"; or brag, "I'm a greasy streak o' lightning" (the last line is from *Negro Workaday Songs*, p. 65). If any conflict comes down to running, there is usually no question that the Negro will win.

So common is the theme of running in Black literature from the slave narratives (whose basic theme is that of the flight from slavery) and the first novel written by a Black American (William Wells Brown's *Clotel*) through the popular works of Richard Wright, Ralph Ellison, and a multitude of others that Phyllis Klotman has entitled her study of Black American literature *Another Man Gone: The Black Runner in Afro-American Literature*. The

"He's Long Gone"

theme continues with the recently published *Brothers and Keepers* by John Edgar Wideman. As one reads each of the many works that focus on this theme, one witnesses repetition after repetition of the scenarios that involve Ralph Ellison's Invisible Man, wherein everyone seems to conspire to "Keep This Nigger-Boy Running."[5] Indeed many of the writers themselves, from Frederick Douglass to Richard Wright, James Baldwin and Eldridge Cleaver, have experienced the dilemma of the man on the run. Several of them fled the American South, and some of them ultimately fled the country.

Thus, as is revealed in both their folklore and their literature, as much pleasure as the Black people might derive from outsmarting white people, there always comes a time when the skill of running is requisite. As the old proverb says, "Whut you don' hab in yo' haid, yuh got ter hab in yo' feet" (*American Negro Folklore*, p. 325). And as a young Black child told Robert Coles in an interview a few years ago: "Legs mean more than hands. So I gives them more attention. If you can run, you're O.K."[6]

Obviously when the Black man speaks of running, he does not always mean it literally. In addition to "putting on my walkin' shoes," he may find that his flight requires that he "hitch up my buggy," "saddle my ole grey mare," "jump a rail," "get a ole Greyhound bus and ride" (all traditional), or "[cool] 'bout hundred-fifteen miles an hour in my / own limousine" ("The Great MacDaddy," *Deep Down*, p. 163). While his travels might take him many places, most of his songs and tales tell of his traveling some road or highway—"a lonesome road," or "a lonesome highway," the "king's highway," or the "gospel highway." The Black runner most often follows the North Star, traveling from South to North, usually leaving towns in Georgia, Arkansas, Alabama, Mississippi (especially Vicksburg and Clarksdale), and other such "mean ole Jim Crow towns," and setting out for New Orleans, Memphis, Nashville, Chicago, New York, Detroit, and St. Louis. The runner's songs frequently depict the horrors of life in the mean old Southern towns and the anticipation of a better life in the North: he's "*sweet* Chicago bound" or he's headed "up north where money grows on trees." In the Black folk tradition, even snakes get out of Mississippi, and God is afraid to travel any further South than Memphis.

Most of their songs and tales allude to, but generally do not detail, the suffering, hardships, and pain that Blacks are trying to escape. Generally there is enough information (coupled with our own knowledge of the history of race relations) to convince us that escape is requisite for survival, and that it is worth the risk of life and limb that it probably entails. Thus the Black man sings, "I'd rather drink muddy water, sleep in a hollow log, than to stay in this here town, treated like a dirty dog" (traditional). He sings, "The devil he thought he had me fast, but I thought I'd break his chains at last" (*Negro Spirituals*, p.23). Blind Lemon Jackson sang, "Gettin' tired of sleepin' in this low-down lonesome cell" (*Blues Fell This Morning*, p. 216).

When the Brileys and their cohorts drove out of Mecklenburg prison and entered that long, lonely, dark country road, they triggered on one level the gut reaction that many Blacks have to the archetypal runner.[7] One must remember that the Black runner, whether he or she be Nat Turner or Harriet Tubman or Frederick Douglass or JoAnne Little or Angela Davis or Stagolee or James Briley, is always labeled and regarded by the system as a fugitive, a desperado, a dangerous criminal, a vicious threat to society; and his flight is always in violation of the established law. Whatever one's view of the individuals involved in the Great Escape, whether one reacted fearfully to the threat posed by those convicted felons or whether one harbored suspicions that perhaps they were victims of an unjust legal system more inclined to execute its poor and Black,[8] there was often, before these balanced considerations, a visceral reaction to the *flight* and a recollection of a host of other runners. And those who recognized themselves most susceptible to the possible loss of their own freedom undoubtedly recognized even more keenly that the fugitive who might generally be judged undeserving craved freedom every bit as much as the runner whom some deemed worthy.

> Inside looking out,
>   I see the happiness
>   and sadness, the hurt

"He's Long Gone"

and pain that everyone feels,
even while here
　　Inside Looking Out . . . .

James Briley, *Fysk Magazine,*
Summer 1984, written before the escape

Very likely they recognized as well that while on one level it may seem blasphemous to link the name of so valiant a heroine as Harriet Tubman with that of a cold blooded murderer, that chain was forged by their respective societies who judged them both the same and hunted them in like manner as similarly dangerous threats to the maintenance of order.

Runagate Runagate

I.

Runs falls rises stumbles on from darkness into darkness
and the darkness thicketed with shapes of terror
and the hunters pursuing and the hounds pursuing
and the night cold and the night long and the river
to cross and the jack-muh-lanterns beckoning beckoning
and blackness ahead and when shall I reach that somewhere
morning and keep on going and never turn back and keep on
　　going

　　Runagate

　　　Runagate

　　　　Runagate

Many thousands rise and go
many thousands crossing over

　　　　　O mythic North
　　　　O star-shaped yonder Bible city

Some go weeping and some rejoicing
some in coffins and some in carriages
some in silks and some in shackles

　　　Rise and go or fare you well

No more auction block for me
no more driver's lash for me

Long Gone

If you see my Pompey, 30 yrs of age,
new breeches, plain stockings, negro shoes;
if you see my Anna, likely young mulatto
branded E on the right check, R on the left,
catch them if you can and notify subscriber.
Catch them if you can, but it won't be easy.
They'll dart underground when you try to catch them,
plunge into quicksand, whirlpools, mazes,
turn into scorpions when you try to catch them.

And before I'll be a slave
I'll be buried in my grave

North star and bonanza gold
I'm bound for the freedom, freedom-bound
and oh Susyanna don't you cry for me

Runagate

Runagate

II.
Rises from their anguish and their power,

Harriet Tubman,

woman of earth, whipscarred,
a summoning, a shining

Mean to be free

And this was the way of it, brethren brethren,
way we journeyed from Can't to Can.
Moon so bright and no place to hide,
the cry up and the patterollers riding,
hound dogs belling in bladed air.
And fear starts a-murbling, Never make it,
we'll never make it. *Hush that now,*
and she's turned upon us, levelled pistol
glinting in the moonlight:
dead folks can't jaybird-talk, she says;
you keep on going now or die, she says.

Wanted   Harriet Tubman   alias The General
alias Moses   Stealer of Slaves

"He's Long Gone"

In league with Garrison   Alcott   Emerson
Garrett   Douglass   Thoreau   John Brown

Armed and known to be Dangerous

Wanted   Reward   Dead or Alive

> Tell me, Ezekiel, oh tell me do you see
> mailed Jehovah coming to deliver me?

Hoot-owl calling in the ghosted air,
five times calling to the hants in the air.
Shadow of a face in the scary leaves,
shadow of a voice in the talking leaves:

> Come ride-a my train

> *Oh that train, ghost-story train*
> *through swamp and savanna movering movering,*
> *over trestles of dew, through caves of the wish,*
> *Midnight Special on a sabre track movering movering,*
> *first stop Mercy and the last Hallelujah.*

> Come ride-a my train

> Mean mean mean to be free.

"It was just like, hey, yawl ain't gon' leave ME in here. You know,
if you got a chance to be free, you aim to take it."

Escapee Derick Peterson
Conversation, June 28, 1985

Long Gone

CHAPTER 2

"They Gone, Jack"

The Escape from Mecklenburg

So many moons ago, I traveled to an unknown place
    And to get there required such a hazardous pace
footsteps a many, doors and keys just chiming
    It's five o'clock, the guard shaking the bars
almost screaming.

There were four dressed in blue, one in white[1]
    Fear is always present, when travel is by night.
"Get up, on the double," the words shouted loud and clear
    "Today is your lucky day, pack your gear."
"Where in the hell am I going?" I asked the wisecracker.
    With a smirking smile on his face, he whispered:
"Mansion in the Back . . ." [Mecklenburg]

Underground tales begin to flash upon my mind
Mecklenburg, Mecklenburg, Mecklenburg,
    That bad ass place, where time is really time.
Men, boys, killers, they all are here
    Some by force, others by will.
The brutality is cruel, insensitivity is the guards' way
    Two broken noses, some bruised skulls, just an ordinary
day.

Larry Batten, Mecklenburg
Composed July 23, 1980
Received Spring 1985

    The Mecklenburg Correctional Center, bane of Virginia's inmates and (until the escape) the pride of its correctional system, was built in stages between 1974 and 1982 at a cost of $20 million to serve as the maximum security facility for the entire correctional system of Virginia.[2] The center began operations in March 1977 with two of the five planned buildings completed.

Mecklenburg Correctional Center, Mecklenburg County, Virginia. Grateful acknowledgment is made to Ben R. Johns, Jr., AIA, Architect, and the Virginia Department of Corrections for permission to use the above drawing.

Touted as a model maximum security prison, it was during the year of the escape one of the most expensive prisons in the country to run, costing the taxpayers of the state $29,176 per inmate in 1983-84, according to an analysis by the State Senate finance committee. The ratio of guards to inmates that was maintained at Mecklenburg (1 to 1.2, "Report of the Mecklenburg Correctional Center Study Committee," p. 121) is one of the highest in the nation.

Mecklenburg is not a stereotypical prison; it is no dismal fortress with lines of prison cells facing each other across endless hallways patrolled by armed guards. Indeed it looks more like a campus, with its two-tiered buildings spread out in a circular manner over a large lawn with woods providing a pastoral backdrop. Each of the five buildings designed to house inmates is basically self-contained, having four control centers, three pods (each pod has twenty-four single-residence cells on the second floor), program space, day rooms, recreation areas, and eating facilities. The prison is designed to accommodate 360 inmates, all of whom are housed in single cells. Each building is entered through double computer-controlled doors operated by guards within central control rooms facing the entrance. When one door is opened, a person enters a sally port; the first door is locked before the second door is unlocked. The central control room also provides a view of each cell. There are four three-story security towers, and the facility is surrounded by link fencing, barbed wire, and coiled razor wire. Virginia prison officials were confident that in Mecklenburg they had achieved an escape-proof facility; when the facility was completed, the assistant superintendent of the prison asserted that the design "is going to make it difficult, next to impossible, for them [prisoners] to start or create any real type of disturbance that we will not be able to deal with" (*Post*, August 12, 1984, p. A–8). And indeed during its seven-plus years of operation before the Great Escape, no successful escape from Mecklenburg ever occurred.

Despite the fact that Mecklenburg is a beautiful, relatively new, apparently secure facility, it has not been without its problems, even before the escape. Designed to house the most dangerous and disruptive of Virginia's prisoners, the population of Mecklenburg consisted of Virginia's most violent inmates at the time of the escape. There are three main categories of prisoners at Mecklenburg: 1) those in the "phase program" (a program designed for disruptive inmates from all state facilities, consisting of special levels designed to reward inmates' progress with additional privileges as a means of encouraging inmates to improve their behavior to the point where they can be returned to the general population in other institutions); 2) those in the "maximum security" unit (inmates who represent a danger to the community or the staff and other inmates; those who have been sentenced to more than fifty years for a violent crime, who represent the threat of potential escape, or who have completed the phase program but cannot be returned to another prison for any reason); and 3) those in a "special purpose" group (inmates who are administrative transfers, investigative holds, in protective custody, or sentenced to death). In addition to these three main categories, there are three other assignment categories: "segregation" (disruptive inmates who do not wish to participate in the phase program); "isolation" (the assignment of an inmate to a cell as punishment for a violation of an institutional rule or procedure); and "mental health" (inmates who have mental health problems which are not so acute as to warrant confinement at Central State Hospital or the Marion Correctional Center).[3] In his report of June 27, 1984, James D. Henderson, consultant from the National Institute of Corrections, described the inmates at Mecklenburg as "a hostile, aggressive, highly dangerous inmate population," and he went on to note, "This writer has rarely seen a facility in which such ungovernable conduct was apparently the norm, with staff and visitors alike subjected to an unusual amount of abuse and danger" (p. 14). The present warden, Toni Bair, observed that on his first visit to Mecklenburg he saw a seething hellhole: "All I could see was flash fires. . . . The inmates had flooded the building. They were screaming and cursing and ranting and raving." He was told that what he was viewing was an everyday occurrence (*TD*, May 26, 1985, p. 1). The center is also dirty and unsanitary, according to James D. Henderson. He noted

that disruptive, uncontrolled inmates have thrown debris and
garbage in most areas of the institution, creating "devastating" (p. 24) and "intolerable" (p. 31) problems to safety and hygiene. Other problems at Mecklenburg cited by various sources include inmate idleness and inadequate supervision.

Mecklenburg's difficulties also include the ready availability of drugs and other contraband. In a shakedown in 1983 one of the Briley brothers was found with sixty-three marijuana cigarettes (*TD*, July 6, 1984, p. B-2). Indeed a few days before the Great Escape, a guard was arrested for providing marijuana to Death Row inmates. A Mecklenburg inmate explained to me the profit to be derived from the drug trade at Mecklenburg: "With the stinking pay they give these officers for having their lives placed in constant danger, they shouldn't be surprised when one of their own accepts to bring reefer in here for the enormous prices that inmates pay for reefer. A forty dollar ounce, (society price), cost an inmate 150 to 200 dollars to have an officer bring it to him. That can result in a guard making $200 profit. Six inmates can get the guard $1,000 clear every two weeks, more than he makes from the state" (letter, March 1985). One death row inmate, Dennis Stockton, alleged that they had wild parties, made wine, and grew marijuana in the cells on Death Row (*Pilot*, September 16, 1984, pp. C-2 and C-11).

According to reports and studies following the escape, the prison has also been plagued with inadequately trained guards, the failure of guards to be familiar with and to follow prescribed procedures, poor supervision and management, and a host of other problems, including most notably impersonal and sometimes hostile relations between guards and inmates. Most newspaper accounts and consultants' reports note the poor quality of interaction between staff and inmates at Mecklenburg, a problem which several suggest contributed to the escape and other later difficulties at the institution. Mecklenburg has experienced more inmate assaults on correctional personnel than any other correctional institution in the state. According to reports, some inmates routinely verbally abuse the staff; throw food, urine, or feces on them; spit on them; hit them; or attack them with weapons.

"They Gone, Jack"

Mecklenburg has also been plagued with accusations of assaults on inmates by guards.

Despite these very serious problems at Mecklenburg, officials never questioned its security. Their confidence that they were prepared to deal with any possible problem continued unabated until the escape on May 31, 1984. Franklin White, public safety secretary, explained to the Virginia House of Delegates appropriations committee on August 20, 1984, that one of the major contributing factors to the success of the escape was that prison officials were suffering a "Titanic Syndrome": they were absolutely comfortable and secure in the belief that Mecklenburg was escape proof. Not only was Mecklenburg not escape proof, it apparently did not provide even minimal security. Studies following the escape unanimously noted a host of design problems that contributed to the escape. Indeed the present warden describes the design as "atrocious" (*TD,* May 26, 1985, p. A-4).

> They put me in that dark dingy cell
> While I was in there, I met my friend
>   named Snake.
> Me and Snake planned a prison
>   break.
> Over the wall through the muddy
>   grass,
> Snake got caught but I was too
>   fuckin' fast.
>
> William Labov, Paul Cohen, Clarence Robins,
> and John Lewis, "Toasts," in *Mother Wit,* p. 343

From the moment they were brought to Mecklenburg, inmates on death row were planning an escape.[4] Indeed even before coming to Mecklenburg, any number of the principals involved in the Great Escape had contemplated, attempted, or even accomplished escape.

> "You've got rabbit in your blood."
>
> Jerry (pseudonym)
> February 28, 1985, Mecklenburg

When the Brileys were at the Richmond city jail before their trials, according to inmate Jerry, they contemplated escape (letter, March

3, 1985). At the time Anthony, the younger brother, was confined
in A-1-L (left side of the first floor of Building A, then reserved
for juveniles) and James and Linwood were in A-2-R, Jerry says
he heard the two older brothers "talking about how easy it was
to cut through the windows in which the metal was not so thick,"
but because they were soon separated they could not get together
to plan the escape. Later when he observed them at Mecklenburg,
working out in the yard outside the Death Row cellblock and
practicing karate, he suspected they were getting in shape for
"something like that. I looked at them and said, 'You've got rabbit
in your blood' " (letter March 3, and conversation, Mecklenburg,
February 28, 1985).

> "Here you are, MacDaddy, here's your coat!"
> I put my hand in my pocket and much to my surprise,
> I put my hand on two forty-fives.
> I throwed them on the judge and made my way to the door.
> As I was leaving, I tipped my hat. . . once more.
> . . . .
> The juries left out, and the broads gave a scream,
> I was cooling 'bout hundred-fifteen miles an hour in my
> own limousine.
>
> "The Great MacDaddy,"
in Deep Down, pp. 162–63

> By the courtroom's surprise that ho pulled two long forty-
>   fives.
> Stag grabbed his forty-five and shot his way to the
>   courtroom do',
> Tipped his hat to all the ladies once mo'
> [went and met a friend]
> With a great big, long, white limousine
> [and drove to their hideout].
>
> "Stag," in S&J, p. 229

Another incident in 1981 at Mecklenburg involving James Briley and Earl Clanton suggests that they might have been planning
escape at that time. On October 8 three women visitors, in a
scenario that seems to have been lifted straight out of a toast (a
long, rhyming, narrative poem, frequently treating the exploits

"They Gone, Jack"

of Baad Niggers), attempted to smuggle a gun, ammunition, and drugs to James Briley and Earl Clanton, who were using home-made tools to cut an opening in the partition to receive the contraband. This attempt was thwarted by guards.

It is difficult to determine with any certainty just when the first idea for the Great Escape occurred. One inmate, whom I shall refer to as Red, told me that he had conceived the idea some years before the escape (conversation, Mecklenburg, February 28, 1985)— and some other prisoners not on Death Row had sug-gested as much before I met Red, who is noted for his ingenuity and inventiveness and who had previously planned and accom-plished two prior escapes, one from Courtland Jail in Southamp-ton County (the site of the Nat Turner rebellion) and another from the Tidewater Correctional Unit in Chesapeake City.[5] "The plans for an escape from Mecklenburg began with Frank Coppola, [the Brileys], and me," Red insisted in a conversation with me on April 29, 1985. Earlier (February 28, 1985), Red had told me that he, Coppola, and the Brileys had met and drawn up plans for the escape. While other inmates have mentioned Coppola's role in the initial plans to me (conversation, June 1985), a Death Row inmate, whom I shall refer to as Bill, insists that Coppola was a racist who would never have planned anything with Blacks (Mecklenburg, August 16, 1985). At some point soon after the conception of the plan, others were included in planning ses-sions. (Coppola was executed in August 1982, almost two years before the escape plans were finalized and effected.) In his news conference on April 16, 1985, James Briley said they had planned the escape for two years. Dennis Stockton, who said he helped to plan the escape but then informed authorities of it, indicated that the first planning meeting for the escape took place in March 1984 and was attended by Willie Lloyd Turner, the Brileys, Earl Clanton, Derick Peterson, Timothy Bunch, Wilbert Lee Evans, Alton Waye, and himself (TD, September 17, 1984, p. B-4).[6] He says that Linwood Briley was the first to suggest a meeting and that he had a plan for the escape.[7] If it is assumed that James Briley's and Red's accounts are accurate, it would appear that

Stockton was simply not aware of initial planning that had occurred before he joined the conspiracy.

Red says that he changed the original plans because he decided they were not workable. They met and considered his changes and decided to go with his revised plans. While Red would not give me many details of their original plans and the specific changes, he did note that they had all agreed that each participant would make his own individual plans for his destination after the escape, and they all planned to go their separate ways. Another point that seemed to have been agreed upon by the planners was that they would not hurt anyone during their escape. Red informed me that he insisted upon that during the planning; and another inmate told me "they vowed not to hurt anybody or kill anybody when they escaped, and that they would do their best to stay out there and show society and themselves that they were still true men and that they could live out a respectful and honest life, without the stigma that was placed on them as mass killers" (State Penitentiary, July 31, 1984). At various points several other inmates were in on the plans or were offered the opportunity to participate; several participants indicated that there were plans for taking as many as sixteen or seventeen inmates,[8] but on the night the escape was accomplished, there were only eight men scheduled to flee. Some sources suggest that those offered the chance to join the group were friends of the Brileys; Lem Tuggle provided the rather unlikely explanation that the choice of the participants was based on whether or not they were guilty of the crimes they were sentenced for. They were all, as far as he knew, innocent, he said (TD, July 10, 1984, p. A-5). Apparently Tuggle was one of the last to be invited to join, as he himself noted following his capture: "I was one of the last ones let in on it. I had only been there for two months" (NL, June 13, 1984, p. 1). Indeed at the time of my interview with Landon he speculated that Tuggle may not have been a part of the *planning*. Tuggle's discussion with me suggests, however, that he was an equal planner from the time he arrived on Death Row a few months prior to the escape (June 28, 1985). Several inmates and a couple

"They Gone, Jack"

of officials intimated to me that Tuggle had been asked to join because he was white and they thought that his being white would offer some protection. A Death Row inmate, whom I shall call Bob, told me, "They had to take a *white* man" (Mecklenburg, February 28, 1985). This view is not corroborated by the accounts of the other conspirators, however. Derick Peterson told me that race was not a consideration and that all three of the white guys on their side of the pod had originally been included in the escape plans (conversation, June 28, 1985).

Although most accounts suggest that the Brileys were the key figures in the escape and my own investigation confirms that they certainly played a major role, there are some detractors. One Death Row inmate, who wishes to remain anonymous, told me, "J.B. and Linwood ain't have enough sense to go around the corner" (summer 1985); another inmate at Mecklenburg wrote me that one Death Row inmate "said the Brileys couldn't have planned their way out of a doghouse. . . . On the night of the escape the Brileys forgot most of the plans" (June 1985).

During their meetings, which sometimes lasted over two hours, the plotters drew tables together, took out law books, and turned the TV up loud so that guards could not hear their deliberations and would be misled into thinking that they were working on their appeals. Jay (pseudonym), who was on the other side of the pod, could not attend the meetings, but he was kept informed through conversations conducted through vents. The escape was originally planned for April, but it was delayed because they needed more weapons, according to Stockton. Peterson, however, told me that their original date was scrapped because he was injured: "Everybody said, 'Naw, man, Badah twisted his ankle [so we can't go today].' So Stockton said, 'If we ain't going today, then I ain't going,' but I think that was just an excuse for him to back out of it anyway" (June 28, 1985).

Obviously the planners had carefully observed and analyzed the habits and personalities of the guards, the procedures followed in the management of the institution, and the design of the physical plant; and they had meticulously and ingeniously planned details of the escape: the ruse to gain access to the control

room, the bomb hoax to get out of the prison, and so on. The
bomb hoax had developed when they considered several plans to
exit the prison after seizing Death Row. At first they had not
planned to try to go through the gate: "We were gon try to get
through the Administration Building" (Peterson), but they were
doubtful that would work. Then they recalled that there had not
been a bomb threat since even the longest-term residents had
been at Mecklenburg: "So we KNEW that Mecklenburg wouldn't
know how to respond to a bomb threat" (Peterson). The last
difficult issue of their escape plan had been resolved. Only minor
details and the calculated creation of a relaxed ambience remained. They even considered details such as the shirt sizes of
the guards to be overpowered (*TD*, June 3, 1984, p. A-4). The
inmates conspired to be model prisoners, winning the confidence
of the officers and causing them to fail to be on their guard. James
Briley said in a press conference on April 16, 1985, that the
escapees, recognizing that the officers at Mecklenburg were "just
computerized to do certain things," had been able to "more or
less [use] their own system and [turn] it against them."[9]

Each of the plotters had specific duties assigned to him by
Linwood Briley, according to some accounts, by general consensus, according to others. At any rate it is clear that long beforehand it had been determined who would hide in the bathroom
and take over the control box, who would monitor the telephone
conversations, who would take the hostages, who would keep
lookouts at varied locations, and so on.[10] Because Stockton frequently left Mecklenburg for hearings, he was more familiar with
the outside. He was thus able to make some suggestions to Linwood Briley, whose original plans revealed his lack of acquaintance with much that had transpired since he had been at
Mecklenburg. Stockton notes that Linwood did not, for example,
know there were chains on the sally port gate. Stockton was
therefore scheduled to plan the escape route and to drive the
getaway car.

Red worked out the plans for making and hiding the shanks
(knives). Some of them had been made with a hacksaw out of
metal hacked away from the thick metal door jambs of his and

Linwood Briley's cells, and then posters were put up to conceal the fact that molding had been removed from the doors. The shanks had been sharpened with a file and on the cell floors. One of the shanks recovered by authorities was a machete-like instrument approximately eighteen inches long. Red showed me how he had hollowed out a section of the bottom metal frame of a window like the one he pointed out to me in the Death Row day room where he stood as we talked, and how he stuck the shanks in there. In addition he used a desk that was similar to a table in the day room at the time of our conversation; the table had a big round piece of wood with a center pole supporting it. He cut a hole in the top of the desk and put the knives down in the hollow pole. Then he sealed the desk and the window with a paste that he made out of paint. He noted that the newspapers had incorrectly indicated that the desk and window had been sealed with papier-mâché. All of the weapons were concealed in Cell 68—his own cell—he noted. They had escaped detection when the cells were searched after the authorities received warnings of the impending escape, and it was not until nine days after the escape that investigators discovered the holes and other incriminating evidence in his cell that indicated the key role he had played in the escape. Red was then moved to another cell.

Some inmates have told me that some of the knives used in the escape were made in the prison maintenance shop and smuggled to Death Row. In a statement from one inmate who claims to have assisted in the making of the weapons, and who is now being held in protective custody, he relates:

> I was working in the supply room at this time [and I made some] blades that cut through walls just like a knife through butter.
> . . . This is the way the weapons were given to inmates. They were tied on the end of a VERY thin wire during the day time by a certain member of the yard crew [inmates allowed to work on the yards] and covered with grass. That night the Death Row inmates would pull the string up and bring the weapons up. Many of the weapons. . . used were actually carried in by hand and handed to the Death Row inmates by other inmates who worked on the yard crew. . . and who worked in Building I.
> Taped statement given to the author in June 1985

Long Gone

The careful plans of the conspirators were not unknown to the prison officials. At least two Death Row inmates had reported the escape plans to their lawyer, who had informed state officials; and Stockton had reported information twice to the assistant warden of Mecklenburg. The Virginia attorney general's office was warned on April 19 of the impending escape. Indeed Landon, who noted that the corrections officials had a "virtual blueprint" of the escape plan, told me that their information even included a warning that one of the prisoners would hide in the bathroom (interview, Richmond, July 12, 1984). Corrections officials were notified and the prison was searched at least twice during the six weeks preceding the escape, with the help of a sketch drawn up by an inmate for the authorities indicating where the weapons were concealed. Using that sketch, authorities closed down the prison the night before the escape and searched for weapons, but none were found.

In the meantime, the machinators were beginning to get nervous and suspicion was aroused among them. By April 16, according to Stockton's diary, James Briley was aware that the officials knew of their plans. Stockton then, according to his account, decided to withdraw from the group plotting the escape. Frightened, after a search of the cellblock by authorities and a lockdown, that the Brileys and others were going to get him because they thought he squealed, Stockton wrote to the assistant warden of Mecklenburg about the concealed weapons. On April 18 there was another shakedown (intensive search) and lockup. Told that he would be killed if he did not go along with the escape plan, Stockton again wrote to the assistant warden and told him about "everything." There was another shakedown, and a great deal of tension and paranoia consequently developed among the plotters.

Despite the reality that news spreads quickly over the prison grapevine (even from one prison to another regardless of the restrictions that would seem to inhibit communication among prisoners in different sections of prisons and in different prisons) and despite the fact that a few of the inmates on Death Row who were privy to the plans for escape had informed their attorneys,

"They Gone, Jack"

rumors of the plans were not widespread throughout the prison as might be expected. Several Mecklenburg inmates, including some on Death Row, told me that they were completely surprised at news of the escape, and not one inmate from the population outside of Death Row claimed to be aware of the planned escape beforehand, through Jerry's own observation convinced him that the Brileys were preparing for an escape: "It was in 1979 . . . I met the Briley brothers. I know they were planning to escape from Death Row simply by the way they worked out on the recreation yard and practiced karate, and because [they were] on Death Row but for the most part because they also contemplated escape on A-2-L" (letter, March 3, 1985). Others who had heard some whisperings about an escape discounted them, since such rumors are routine.

> "I'm here today, Lawd, but tomorrow
>   I'll be gone,
> I'm here today, Lawd, but tomorrow
>   I'll be gone."
>
> Folk blues, from Alan Lomax, "I Got the Blues," *Mother Wit*, p. 474

It was rumored that while the planning was a group effort, only the Brileys knew the precise night that the escape would take place.

> "John, John, tonight.
> John, John, tonight."
>
> A signal by which slaves communicated
> that an escape was to take place that night, *S&J*, p. 185

At about 6 PM on the evening of May 31, 1984, the twelve inmates from the right side of C Pod on the second floor of Building No. 1 (including Willie Turner, Dennis Stockton, Charles Sylvester Stamper, Derick Lynn Peterson, Earl Clanton, Jr., Alton Waye, James D. Briley, Linwood Briley, Wilbert Lee Evans, Dana Ray Edmonds, Timothy Dale Bunch, and Lem Davis Tuggle, Jr.) were taken to the recreation area under the supervision of Officers James Fitts and Sandy Walker.[11]

At 7:23 Cpl. Harold Crutchfield came to the recreation yard and escorted Red and Dennis Stockton back to the right wing of

C Pod. Red, following the plan, returned early to get the weapons out and also, according to Peterson, got some tape from downstairs. Red and Stockton were recorded as having entered their cells, though inmates claim that they were not placed in their cells and some documents note that they were taken to the day room. Meanwhile other inmates in the left wing of C Pod were in the day room area of their pod. At about 8 PM the two officers who were supervising those on the recreation area escorted the remaining ten back to the right wing of C Pod. When the group entered the foyer outside C Pod, Earl Clanton slipped into the employee's restroom, which is located just about six feet across from the C Pod control area, where he remained until close to 9 PM. That Clanton was able to conceal himself in this way raised several questions. In the first place prisoners were counted when they went out and when they returned. This was a regulation that some inmates say was religiously followed. One Death Row inmate in an anonymous letter, to the *News Leader*, June 18, 1984, (p. 1) charged, "Either the count going out or coming back in should have been off. I would be inclined to look into someone's bank account over this one mistake." That same writer adds, "To tell you the truth, I can't understand why no one noticed Clanton was missing. He's a very colorful person around here. Not seeing him is like an alarm to problems."

In the meantime Cpl. Harold Crutchfield and Officer James Fitts were working to unlock the door to a pipe closet in the cellblock area to correct a plumbing problem reported by an inmate on the right side of C Pod. At almost the same time Nurse Ethel Barksdale, who had entered Death Row to dispense medications, attempted to get into the guards' restroom to get some water and Officer Sandy Walker attempted to use the restroom, but neither could open the door. Officer Walker informed Officer Ricardo Holmes, who was in charge of the control room, that the door was jammed, but apparently nothing was done about investigating the problem, though one report indicates that Holmes tried to open the door. An inmate provided Nurse Barksdale water from his cell, and she continued distributing medication, accompanied by Officer Donald Gentry. At this time the prisoners

"They Gone, Jack"

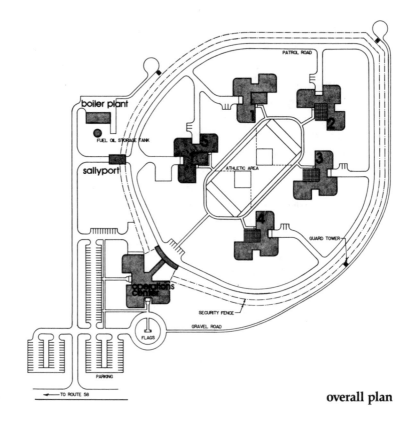

overall plan

Plans of Mecklenburg Correctional Center. Drawings by Ben R. Johns, Jr., AIA, Architect.

Long Gone

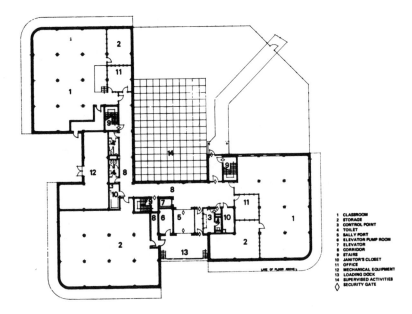

housing unit, first floor

1 CLASSROOM
2 STORAGE
3 CONTROL POINT
4 TOILET
5 SALLY PORT
6 ELEVATOR PUMP ROOM
7 ELEVATOR
8 CORRIDOR
9 STAIRS
10 JANITOR'S CLOSET
11 OFFICE
12 MECHANICAL EQUIPMENT
13 LOADING DOCK
14 SUPERVISED ACTIVITIES
◊ SECURITY GATE

housing unit, second floor

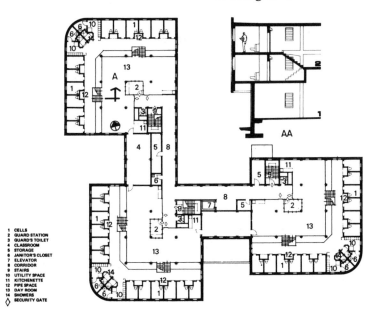

1 CELLS
2 GUARD STATION
3 GUARD'S TOILET
4 CLASSROOM
5 STORAGE
6 JANITOR'S CLOSET
7 ELEVATOR
8 CORRIDOR
9 STAIRS
10 UTILITY SPACE
11 KITCHENETTE
12 PIPE SPACE
13 DAY ROOM
14 SHOWERS
◊ SECURITY GATE

AA

"They Gone, Jack"

in the right wing of the pod were in the day room area. Somewhere around 8:40 Jay called from the left side of C Pod day room and asked Officer Ricardo Holmes to pass a book to James Briley. Officer Holmes unlocked the door of the control room and stepped out to hand the material to Briley, at which point Clanton dashed from the restroom into the control room, and threw the switches to open the doors to both wings of C Pod. At the same time Red, Derick Peterson, and other inmates, some armed, attacked Fitts and Crutchfield, who were working on the plumbing. Officer Holmes meanwhile wrestled with Clanton in the control room and, according to at least one witness, almost had him out of the door when James and Linwood Briley rushed in with a long shank and quickly subdued Holmes. The altercation was witnessed by Officer Sandy Walker, stationed on the inside of the left wing in C Pod, but he was quickly taken captive by Jay. Officer Fitts and Cpl. Crutchfield were overpowered by Red and Peterson. Officer Fitts was forced to remove his outer clothing and was bound, blindfolded, and compelled to lie on the floor. Crutchfield was not bound but was stripped of his outer clothes and forced to lie on the floor of the bottom tier of the right wing of C Pod. Officer Walker was taken hostage by Jay, stripped, bound at the hands and feet, blindfolded, and forced to lie on the floor. All of the guards were made to lie in areas where they were not visible from the control area or the foyer. One of the inmates, clad in a guard's uniform, took over the control box, from which he controlled all the doors. The rebels then confined nine of the inmates on the left side of the pod in the dishwasher room. Two inmates from that side (Jay and Willie Leroy Jones) were participants. The anonymous prisoner in his letter to the NL notes that there was no resistance to the inmate who ordered them in the dishwasher room: "He was carrying so many shanks that he kept dropping them. None of us said no to him" (NL, p. 3). Bob, who was also locked in the dishwasher room, told me that he was afraid at first and that he and several others hoped that the rebels would get away: "I hoped they would get away because I was afraid of what would happen if they came back" (Mecklenburg, February 28, 1985).

Long Gone

At about 8:50 Cpl. Crutchfield was moved to the day room. James Briley called Lt. Larry Hawkins and left a message for him to call the day room of C Pod. When Lt. Hawkins called, James Briley forced Cpl. Crutchfield to request that Lt. Hawkins, the watch commander, report to C Pod to assist a wounded inmate. Lt. Hawkins, busy elsewhere, sent Lt. Milton Crutchfield. In the meantime the inmates had the TV turned up loud so that officers entering the area would not become suspicious. At about this time Officer Donald Gentry went to C Pod to get an elevator key to escort Nurse Barksdale to the first floor. He was taken hostage by Tuggle and Jones, carried to the lower tier, stripped, bound, and blindfolded. Nurse Barksdale went back to C Pod to see what was taking Gentry so long, and she saw someone in a guard's uniform approaching her. She walked toward him. It was inmate Peterson, who grabbed her and pulled out a knife. She pleaded for her life. Her captor advised her to shut up. He took her to Cell 68. Clanton came in and told her she had twenty seconds to take her clothes off. Bill (pseudonym) intervened and asked Clanton to give her a blanket. Then she said when Bill left, Clanton tied her and began to molest her with his hands and Linwood Briley also entered and touched her. At 9:10 PM Lt. Crutchfield entered Building No. 1 and went to the C Pod by way of the stairwell. When he entered the foyer he was captured by Peterson, taken to the bottom tier of the right wing of C Pod, stripped, bound, and left with the other guards. At 9:12 Officer John Mayo was taken hostage in the corridor between B Pod and C Pod and was stripped, bound, and blindfolded and forced to lie on the floor. Hearing the commotion, Officer Eugene Chavis exited B Pod and, upon seeing the inmates in the corridor, attempted to return to B Pod but was taken hostage by Tuggle and Clanton, carried to the lower tier of C, stripped, bound, blindfolded, and put on the floor. At 9:13 Lt. Larry Hawkins, the watch commander, who had been unsuccessful in his attempts to call to check on the situation, went to the building. When he walked through the bottom door, he noticed Peterson dressed in a guard's uniform: "He saw me in a uniform, and he just stared, he just stood there and looked, and I just stood there and looked at him.

"They Gone, Jack"

He was between doors, and. . . somebody said, 'Get him! Go get him! You can't let him get away now.' He couldn't get out because he was stuck between doors" (Peterson, June 28, 1985). Like Lt. Crutchfield, Lt. Hawkins was unable to escape because the bottom door to the stairwell closes and electronically locks behind anyone entering. Inmates Clanton and Tuggle grabbed him and threatened to kill him; Hawkins pleaded for his life. He was stripped and taken to the holding area with the other hostages. Meanwhile Cpl. Prince Thomas, looking for Lt. Hawkins, entered Building No. 1 at 9:28. When Thomas saw the control room manned by an inmate, he ran back down the stairs, attempting three times to contact master control by radio, but he too was trapped by the automatic electronic doors and taken captive by James Briley. He was hustled to the lower tier, stripped of his outer clothing, bound at the hands, and forced to lie on the floor. Meanwhile Sgt. Charlie Holmes received a radio command to call #166, the day room of C Pod. Unable to get an answer on #166, he called the control room and was told by the inmate there to report to C Pod. When he entered, he was taken hostage by Jay and Tuggle, led to the lower tier, stripped of his outer clothing, bound at the hands, and locked in the janitor's closet, where most of the other hostages had been moved by this time. At 10:30 Nurse Maude Boyd, apparently concerned about Nurse Barksdale, went to Building No. 1. She was captured at the C Pod door by Turner and Clanton, placed in Cell 70, and bound. She was not, however, disrobed. About this time inmate Bill was ordered into his cell by James Briley and locked up. Bill told me he cooperated because he did not want to incite those desperate men to any violent act. He said he told the inmates in the guard tower to lock the doors as soon as the escapees went out of the cellblock because he knew that if they were forced to return to the pods, someone would be hurt.

Within a period of one hour and fifty-eight minutes twelve guards and two nurses were taken hostage, ten of them within a span of only thirty-four minutes, and five of those within a span of three minutes. The hostages were bound with "pieces of string and torn sheets and stuff, and we used their own handcuffs on

1985). Some were muffled with pieces of sheet. At first, Peterson told me, the rebels had planned to tape up their mouths and eyes. They did put something over the heads of their first captives, but they later took that off. The fourteen hostages were taken and secured with no injuries and, according to some reports, very few threats. While obviously being grabbed by convicted felons and having an eighteen-inch long shank held against one's throat is intimidation enough, Warden Gary L. Bass indicated that the rebels used direct threats only three times: to force a guard to call the watch commander, to force the captive commander to order the van and to order the key control-room guard to leave her post, and to force that guard to show them how to open the gates to the yard (*TD*, June 8, 1984). According to some reports, the whole operation was smooth, orderly, professional; other witnesses described the behavior of the rebels as wild, chaotic, confused.

The whole experience was naturally a frightening one for the hostages. Several of them later described their experiences to the *News Leader* reporters (June 4, 1984). One noted, "They picked me up by my arms and legs. I thought they were going to bash my brains out against the wall and I started to pray. . . . Instead they crammed my body between the death row cells amongst the plumbing fixtures." Others told of the fear of having shanks held against their throats, being threatened with death, begging for their lives. Some vowed never to return to Mecklenburg Correctional Center.

Inmates Wilbert Lee Evans and Willie Lloyd Turner were credited with calming the escapees throughout the takeover. Turner cautioned them that they had promised that there would be no bloodshed. Both men frequently checked on the women hostages and prevented them from being abused. Evans said he tried to calm the hysterical hostages and got permission to loosen their bonds, remove tape from their faces, and give them water. He got mattresses and pillows for them. One guard held hostage insisted, "I do know I owe my life, as do all the others, to Evans and Turner. . . . They [the escaping inmates] would have killed

"They Gone, Jack"

every damn one of us" (*NL*, June 4, 1984). Several sources suggest that Evans prevented the nurse from being raped. Evans told me that he knows the woman would have been raped had he not intervened: "I told [Clanton] if he wanted to be regarded as a man, he ought to act like a man, and a real man wouldn't treat a woman like that" (February 28, 1985). The *Times-Dispatch* (June 10, 1984) reported that when Evans objected to the escapees undressing the woman, he was told that they had to do it to keep her from running away, and Evans replied, "That white woman ain't going anywhere." The hostage was not white, but Black. The uncorrected impression, however, served to reinforce that dominant obsession of Southern racists that maintains the myth that the first thing the Black male will do when he is free to do so is to rape the white woman. The error clearly served to exacerbate the fears of the public of the dangerous Black beasts turned loose to threaten and ravage Southern white womanhood.[12]

Now that the inmates had captured the officers in charge, according to plans, the rest of their plot to get out of the building was easy. As Peterson told me, "The first thing we had to do was to get the officers in charge; once we got the officers in charge of things, we called the shots—but they think it's coming from the commanding officer. . . . After we got all the white shirts, as we call them, the commanding officers (the lieutenants, and the captains and the sergeants—they dress in white shirts—the rest of the officers, they dress in blue shirts)—once we got all of them, like I say, we could call the shots."

And call the shots they did. At about 10:35, Officer Corlene Thomas, who was operating the main control in Building No. 1, received a call directing her that she was needed elsewhere and that a man was being sent to relieve her. She thought Lt. Hawkins made the call, but it was later surmised that Peterson, disguising his voice by placing a towel over the phone, was the caller. Some of the inmates, who had previously changed into guards' uniforms, went down to the first floor on the elevator. Peterson went up to the control room and informed Officer Thomas that he was there to relieve her. When she opened the control room doors, he overpowered and handcuffed her. Other inmates forced her to show them how to operate the control panel to open the exit door from Building No. 1, after which they put her in the control room restroom.

Peterson, now in command of the main control box, awaited word from his co-conspirators upstairs, when something happened that might have foiled their plans. "I get a phone call, right. And I'm thinking it was coming from upstairs. I JUMP on the phone, and you know say, like, 'Yo, what's up?' And then the officer say, 'Well, who is this? WHO is this? I'm looking for so and so.' He asked asked me where was the officer at. I said, 'I've relieved her; she gone.' He said, 'Where has she gone?' I said I didn't know where she was gone." Following that unsettling call, Peterson received another call, "say everybody ready to come downstairs, right, so I got to press a button to open the door right, so I press the button." Then he received more upsetting news: Jay and Red weren't going. James Briley reportedly went back upstairs to get them, but they were firm in their resolve not to go.

In the meantime, according to official reports, Lt. Hawkins had been forced to call Officer Barry Patillo to request that a van from the boiler plant be sent to the sally port gate to remove a bomb (Peterson recalled disguising his voice and making that call). Officer Susan Fields, who was assigned to the tower opposite the sally port, was called and told, "We have an emergency," and instructed to leave both sally port gates open.

At about 10:31, Officer Patillo had taken a new, blue van to the sally port and called C Pod to so inform them. He thought he was speaking to Officer Gentry and Lt. Hawkins, but he probably talked to an inmate. About 10:38 Officer Patillo, considering the possibility of damage to a good vehicle, decided to call for an older van. The original new blue van was returned to the boiler plant, and an older *white* van was delivered, ironically in keeping with the folk tradition (Stag makes his getaway in a "great big, long, white limousine" [*S&J*, p. 229]).

Tuggle informed me in our conversation of July 8, 1985, that at this time advice from an unlikely source circumvented a serious flaw in their plans. They were not planning to leave the peniten-

"They Gone, Jack"

tiary until almost 12 o'clock, but one of the captured officers warned them that they had better get out quickly "because the white shirts would be coming in soon." The new shift that comes in at 11:30 PM would probably have foiled their escape. When I asked why the officer would volunteer that helpful information, Tuggle laughingly explained, "He wanted us out of there." Evidently the officer, like some of the inmates, feared the consequences if the escapees were thwarted.

The inmates, dressed in ill-fitting guards' uniforms[13] and riot gear with helmets and gas masks, which served to disguise them, hustled a television set covered with a blanket out the exit door directly adjacent to the control area of Building No. 1. Guy (pseudonym) opened the door for the inmates from the main control in Building No. 1. The escapees had not previously planned for anyone to perform this crucial task, but at the last minute they had delegated the task to someone whom they could trust to do it (Tuggle). Peterson recalls, "I was the first one to walk through the gate. I was ahead of everybody else, . . . and I was like clearing the way, [yelling] 'O.K., everybody, get back! We've got a bomb.' " Officer Patillo complied. Instanteously, Linwood and James Briley, Tuggle, Jones, and Clanton dashed across the yard to the sally port, two of them carrying a stretcher with the "bomb," while the other four sprayed it with a fire extinguisher. The inmates ran the last few yards to where the van stood waiting.

> Swing low, sweet chariot, coming for to carry me home;
> Swing low, sweet chariot, coming for to carry me home.
> I looked over Jordan and what did I see,
> Coming for to carry me home.
>
> Traditional

> The gospel train is coming
> . . . .
> Get on board, children, get on board.
>
> Traditional

This was the first time during the whole escapade that at least one of the inmates felt that their plan would work; when he saw

10, 1984, p. A-5). When I asked Peterson if he thought the plot
was going to work at that point, he laughed, "Me, myself—no.
But it was worth a try, right."

The men threw the stretcher into the open rear doors and
sprinted in after it, while Linwood Briley took the driver's seat
and drove out through the open gates. Over his guards' radio,
Linwood Briley ordered, "Close the gates!" They sped away from
Mecklenburg at 10:47 PM.

> "I was cooling 'bout hundred-fifteen miles an hour
>   in my own limousine."
>   "The Great McDaddy," *Deep Down*, p. 163

Shortly after the getaway, Guy returned to C Pod. Red and Jay
changed back into their prison garb. About twenty minutes after
the escapees left Building No. 1 and eighteen minutes after they
left the prison, Jay opened the doors to the stairwell, allowing Lt.
Hawkins, who had been brought down the stairs by the escapees
and locked in the stairwell, to return to C Pod. This delay in
freeing the hostages was a decision of those inmates who remained and was not something that the escapees had planned,
Tuggle and other inmates who did not escape later told me. Tuggle
noted that he and the other escapees were grateful that the guys
on Death Row decided to keep things locked down for a while to
give them the headstart that clearly contributed to the success of
their escape. The other hostages and some prisoners, including
Evans, were then freed. Evans then broke into the laundry room
by bending back a door and screen and helped to untie the
hostages. Then, according to Evans, "they thanked me for everything I done for saving their lives and they shook my hand."

The scene on Death Row at this point was farcical, according
to several inmates with whom I have talked and corresponded.
When the guards were released, there was a mad rush by the
unclothed men and women to find clothes. Several of their gar-
ments had been thrown in the pod area and the embarrassed
guards were scrambling around to find their uniforms, some of

"They Gone, Jack"

them resorting to putting on inmates' clothing (letter from Mecklenburg, July 21, 1985). It was some time before new guards came in and any semblance of control was resumed over Death Row.

Lt. Hawkins informed master control of the escape at 11:15 PM.

After the struggle between Clanton and Officer Holmes in the control tower at the beginning of the takeover, the guards had apparently offered little resistance. Although the newspapers at first reported that the guards were armed with "stun guns," Robert Landon informed me that that was not true; their only weapons were night sticks. Inmates added that the guards also had mace. When one considers the weapons the inmates had (Will recalled that each of the inmates active in the uprising had at least two shanks) and the advantage of surprise that they enjoyed, it seems prudent for the guards to have submitted. Even one of the inmates noted that "none of the officers resisted. And I cannot blame any of them" (*NL*, June 18, 1984, p. 3).

Several of the inmates who had been offered the option of joining the escapees remained on Death Row. Some obviously thought there was little chance for success and chose not to take the chance of being maimed or killed in an escape attempt. Others informed me that they did not want to jeopardize their chances for their appeals because they felt they had good cases. The most surprising withdrawal, however, was Red. Instrumental in planning the escape, active throughout, largely in controlling possible violence and reassuring the guards, Red chose not to leave with his cohorts but rather stayed behind and untied the guards. Although he would not tell me what specifically motivated him to decide not to leave, he did inform me that he had not decided whether he was going to leave or not, even after the escape was initiated: "I didn't know until the last minute that I wasn't going. It was a lot of reasons [that I decided not to go]" (May 29, 1985). Another reason to be inferred from our conversation was the recognition that had he gone he might have been viewed as the most dangerous felon. Given his previous escapes, the fact that he was the oldest, the fact that he was the most experienced, and the fact that he was the one who had initiated the plans and concealed the weapons, he noted, the officials might immediately have recognized his key role: "If I had went, I would have caught the flack." As it was, the Brileys caught the flack, and a part of catching the flack, according to Red and numerous other inmates, was that they provoked an intense fear that led authorities to rush their execution. (One inmate told me that Red said "he don't want to be a DEAD legend, like the Brileys" [letter from Mecklenburg, June 27, 1985]). Three other inmates who had been active in planning and executing the escape also chose not to leave.

No escape of this magnitude had ever been accomplished from the death row of any prison in this country. Previous escapes of condemned men from Virginia prisons occurred before they were transferred to Death Row. These include the escape by Red from Courtland Jail in Southampton County and the escape of two whites, Walter Legenza and Robert Mais, who shot their way out of the Richmond city jail on September 29, 1934, seriously injuring three policemen, one of whom died four days later. Like the Great Escape, that escape precipitated the largest search Virginia had seen since the Nat Turner rebellion and prompted extensive investigations and vehement criticisms of the correctional system.[14]

While the Mecklenburg Death Row was being controlled by inmates in an unprecedented takeover, and six Death Row inmates were speeding away from the institution in a record-breaking escape, most of the rest of the prison was completely unaware of what was happening. One inmate who was there at the time in Building No. 1 in isolation (the same building in which the Death Row is located) learned of the escape only when later that night he heard the excited voices of inmates yelling, "They gone, Jack!"

CHAPTER 3

The Men on the Loose

Sketches of the Escapees

The six men who drove away from Mecklenburg Correctional Center's Death Row at 10:47 PM on the night of May 31, 1984, were convicted of or implicated in some of the most heinous crimes committed in Virginia over the preceding five years, including twenty murders and four rapes, as well as a host of other offenses such as robbery, sodomy, possession of a firearm, abduction, and malicious wounding. The Briley brothers, James and Linwood, the most notorious of the group, were alleged to have been involved in thirteen murders. They were tried and convicted (or in one instance found "not innocent"), between them, of a total of eight murders.

> Says the judge he found me guilty,
>   and the clerk he wrote it down
> Says the judge he found me guilty
>   and the clerk he wrote it down
> Says the judge, "Tell everybody that,
>   Lawd, you' chain gang boun'."
>
> "Chain Gang Blues" (recorded by Kokomo Arnold in 1935)
> from *Blues Fell This Morning*, p. 212

Earl Clanton, Jr. (thirty at the time of the escape) had been on Mecklenburg's Death Row since March 13, 1981. He received the death sentence for the November 16, 1980, murder of Wilhelmina Smith, a thirty-nine-year-old librarian at A.P. Hill Elementary School in Petersburg, Virginia. Clanton had been paroled a few months earlier for his role in a 1972 murder and robbery of a New Jersey woman. In April he had escaped from custody in the Petersburg circuit court during a trial for malicious wounding.

The next time law officials saw him was when they found him under the bed of Miss Smith, who had been strangled with a belt and stabbed as she struggled with her assailant. They recovered one blood-covered $5.00 bill and three $1.00 bills that he had presumably taken from the victim.

Willie Leroy Jones (twenty-five at the time of the escape) had been on Mecklenburg's Death Row since March 15, 1984. He was convicted of killing and robbing an elderly Charles City couple (Graham Adkins, seventy-seven, and Myra Adkins, seventy-nine), on May 13, 1983. The couple had retired the previous year after running a small country store for over thirty years. Jones had worked in Richmond with the Adkins' son, who shortly before the murders had allowed Jones to live with him in his home in Charles City after Jones was laid off from his job. During the two weeks Jones lived with their son, Mr. and Mrs. Adkins became friendly with him and Mrs. Adkins read the Bible with him. She frequently asked her son about Jones after he returned to Richmond to live with his sister. According to statements he made to the police, testimony in the preliminary hearing, and testimony introduced during his trial, Jones, disguised in a wig, returned to the Adkins' home on May 13. He told them he was an undercover policeman looking for missing children, and to substantiate this sham he produced pictures that he had cut out of a yearbook. After he gained entrance into the home, he pulled out a gun, pointed it at Mr. Adkins' head, and pulled the trigger, but it failed to fire. The elder Adkins, apparently thinking it was a joke, laughed and said, "Bang, you have got me." Jones reportedly retorted, "What the fuck are you laughing at?"[1] and pulled the trigger again, shooting him in the head. Mrs. Adkins came into the room, and Jones made her take him to their safe, which was variously reported to have contained between $35,000 and $45,000. He took his wig off, revealing who he was, told Mrs. Jones not to worry, that he wouldn't hurt her, tied her up, stuffed her mouth with something (apparently a sock), taped her mouth, handed her a Bible, and asked her to pray for him. He is quoted as saying that while he was trying to break into the safe with a hammer and by shooting it, he was praying for forgiveness.[2] After

Long Gone

opening the safe, he shot Mrs. Adkins in the face, left her body in a closet, and set the house on fire. She died of smoke inhalation. Jones then hitchhiked back to Richmond and went on a spending spree, casually disbursing musty old bills in generous tips and extravagant purchases that would later be recalled at his trial. He spent two nights in a Richmond hotel and a motel, took a taxi to Washington, and flew to Honolulu. He registered in Honolulu's biggest hotel, the Aloha Surf Hotel, purchased expensive designer clothes, fine jewelry, and a car. One week after the murders, he was arrested at the Aloha Surf, where authorities confiscated a briefcase with $28,733 in old money. Jones, a neat, clean-cut young man with whom I spoke briefly at Mecklenburg, generally acquiesced to James Briley, from whom he seemed to await his cues.

Derick Lynn Peterson (twenty-two at the time of the escape) had been on Mecklenburg's Death Row since November 4, 1982. He received the death sentence for the February 7, 1982, murder of Howard Kauffman, the office manager of a Hampton supermarket from which Peterson took $4,000 in checks and cash. He was also convicted and sentenced for armed robbery the month before the murder of Kauffman and for robbery and abduction the day after. The object of some ribbing since his recapture, he shrugs it off with good humor and laughs about some of the incidents of his escape and recapture.

Lem Davis Tuggle, Jr. (thirty-two at the time of the escape and the only white who escaped) had been on Mecklenburg's Death Row since March 26, 1984. He was sentenced to death for the June 1, 1983, murder of Jessie Geneva Havens, a fifty-two-year-old woman whom he reportedly escorted from a dance at the American Legion hall near Marion, Virginia. The partly-clad body of the victim, who had been bitten, sodomized, and shot in the heart, was thrown into a ditch less than half a mile from the spot in Smyth County where the body of a seventeen-year-old girl whom Tuggle had earlier been convicted of raping and murdering was found in 1971. In 1972 he had been sentenced to twenty years in jail for second degree murder. He was paroled in 1981, returned to prison for violation of parole, and then paroled again 104 days before his arrest for the Havens death. During his first murder trial he escaped from Smyth County Jail by sticking a spoon in a guard's back and telling him it was a knife. Later he escaped from Bland Correctional Farm. In addition to the death sentence, Tuggle also received sentences for sodomy and the use of a firearm in the commission of a felony. Since the escape, Tuggle has been portrayed by the media and some investigators as a bungling incompetent taken along for the ride and for the protection his whiteness offered the group. One investigator, who asked not to be identified, told me when commenting on their ability to extract information from him, "Tuggle wasn't the brightest guy to come down the road" (June, 1985). In my conversations with him I found him a much more sophisticated and perceptive person than that widespread image suggests. He seemed to have had more definite plans than the other escapees for seeking a secure haven where he could enjoy an extended freedom. My impressions are more consistent with those of the Smyth County commonwealth attorney, who described him as "a calm, cool and collected individual" (*TD*, June 9, 1984). Tuggle has publicly revelled in the role of outlaw and desperado more than any of the other escapees and has viewed events surrounding his sentencing and escape satirically and boastfully. The pride he felt in inspiring such a large scale search, arousing such fear, and achieving such notoriety is evident in his many public statements. When he was captured following his escape, he enthusiastically volunteered his identity: "I'm Lem Tuggle. I think you'll find I'm wanted pretty bad by the people back in Virginia" (*TD*, June 10, 1984). He proudly related how the arresting officer reacted after finding out who he was: he "fell back in his car and said, 'Oh, my God, what am I going to do?' " (*TD*, July 10, 1984). Later, one FBI agent told me, he bragged, "I'm the only white man ever to escape from Mecklenburg" (anonymous, June, 1985). In his response to my first letter to him he informed me of the number of requests he was receiving for interviews. He later told me that the owner of the pickup truck he drove to Vermont had refused an offer of $20,000 for it and had chosen to restore it and keep it himself. He also informed me that he had been told that the Red Mills Gift Shop in Vermont,

Long Gone

which he robbed, has a neon sign proclaiming, "Lem Tuggle stopped here." He noted further that since his capture, several guards at the penitentiary had requested his autograph (conversation, Richmond, July 8, 1985). Tuggle also reveals a sense of macabre humor: when he was sentenced to death, he reportedly quipped, "I guess you can call me 'Sparky' now" (*TD*, June 9, 1984, p. A-5; Sparky is the term popularly used by inmates to refer to the electric chair). He sports a tatoo on his left forearm that reads, "Born to Die." (Tuggle later was involved in a foiled escape from the Mecklenburg Correctional Center on November 27, 1985.)

Tuggle's loquacious pleasure at being in the limelight offered a marked contrast to the public reserve and silence maintained by the Briley brothers, neither of whom granted any interviews to the press until a couple of days before their imminent executions. And even then Linwood refused to comment on the escape at all and James's comments were reserved and only mildly hinting at the traditional Badman's pleasure in his exploits without any of the expected, traditional bravado. Indeed Linwood expressed dismay at the fact that the escape had motivated T-shirts, bumper stickers, and songs: "I wish they'd cut that out. . . People have placed us on the celebritylike status, you know. I try to put that aside because there's no thrill behind it" (*TD*, September 30, 1984, p. 1).

Several of those who met, talked with, and knew the Briley brothers at various periods of their lives described them as bright, innovative, mannerly, reserved, even dignified. Three of their teachers characterized them as "fine young fellows—as polite and courteous as they could be," "quiet and mannerable," and "no discipline problem" (interviews, Richmond, August 19, 1985). One noted that they were extremely cooperative young men who would do whatever they were asked and who were pleasant, even when being reprimanded. Reverend Odie Brown, a prominent Richmond minister who also serves as a chaplain at the Virginia State Penitentiary and who visited Linwood daily, quoted the former editor of the *Afro* as calling him a gentleman, and Brown concurred, saying that in his experience with him he was "the

The Men on the Loose

all-American boy" (interview, Richmond, June 17, 1985). Linwood's lawyer, Deborah Wyatt, characterized him as intelligent and personable (*NL*, October 16, 1984, p. 6). Kathi King, the Virginia State Penitentiary's operations officer whose duty included receiving and attempting to facilitate the last requests of the Brileys, described them as "very respectful" (interview, Virginia State Penitentiary, Richmond, August 14, 1985). People who knew them in Philadelphia during their escape described them as "nice guys" who were hard working and helpful (*NL*, June 21, 1984, p. 4). Several people recalled that the brothers were soft spoken and not given to heavy drinking and profanity; Reverend Brown was struck by the fact that he "*never* [heard] him [Linwood] curse" (interview, June 17, 1985). Inmates at the State Penitentiary and at Mecklenburg, some of whom were friends of the Brileys before their incarceration and others who had met them in prison, generally spoke very positively of them. Generally these inmates paint a picture of men who were intelligent, friendly, helpful, generous, popular, and respected. Derick Peterson, a fellow escapee, proclaimed, "They were good people" (conversation, June 28, 1985). Many of their fellow inmates had doubts about their guilt.

Although no inmates suggested that they were afraid of the Brileys, and although there were few suggestions that the brothers threatened or bullied their comrades, there are many subtle indications that others were intimidated by them. After describing Linwood's initial friendliness to him when he first arrived on Death Row, his continual generosity to him, and his honesty in dealing with others, Dennis Stockton concludes that he is "not someone to mess with" (*Pilot*, September 16, 1984, p. C-4). He goes on to say that James Briley is "possibly the smartest and shrewdest man here," but concludes "I wouldn't want him for an enemy."

It appears that at least some guards were inclined to fear the Brileys and some to acquiesce to them. Jerry, an inmate, told me that guards at the Richmond jail were "so afraid of them that they would slide their food to them under the dirty and filthy door" (letter, March 3, 1985). Guards at Mecklenburg reportedly delivered marijuana to them regularly, overlooked certain infractions on their part, and allowed them some privileges denied to others. Stockton claims in his diary that a guard delivered shanks to Linwood and helped him hide a shank during a shakedown. Indeed the escape was facilitated by a guard's stepping out of the control box, a clear infraction of procedures, to hand a book to James Briley. The prison grapevine at the State Penitentiary reports that James Briley arranged a conjugal visit with his wife on Death Row and that a high ranking official lost his job as a result (conversation with Virginia State Penitentiary inmate, July 21, 1985). However, during my conversation with Ms. King, who said she was present during the one contact visit James Briley had with his wife on the Sunday before his execution, she denied that it was a conjugal visit (August 14, 1985).

The Brileys' control of any situation and any group of which they were a part has been constantly noted. Reverend Brown told me that sometimes he would have to wait for Linwood's attention as he completed some activity in which he was involved in an almost ritualistic way before turning his attention to his visitor: "[Linwood] was sort of like a computer. He did things . . . by rote. For example, the days that he took a shower, sometimes I was down there. He would come out the shower, would dry himself off—he was very fond of his hair. He would towel dry his hair; he would comb his hair. And not saying too much to me. He would plait that hair in the back and put his stocking cap on. And what was interesting, he always rubbed down in cocoa butter. After that he would say, 'Guard, I'd like to have one coffee, two sugars, and a cigarette.' And *then* he'd talk to me. I think he was so much in control of himself and of the people around him until he just knew you'd be there." Brown went on to note that one day he said to Linwood, "You know, you got me hypnotized," and Linwood replied, "Yeah, I can do that to people." He said Linwood had told him the day before his execution, "You never let situations control you, you control them."

In interviews with the *Times-Dispatch* prior to the scheduled execution of Linwood Briley in August, some neighbors who live in the quiet, lower-middle-class Highland Park neighborhood in

Richmond's North Side where the brothers grew up expressed a confidence in his innocence. While the neighbors acknowledged that the incarcerated Briley brothers were into petty crimes and fencing, they insisted that they were not capable of the vicious crimes of which they were convicted. One friend described Linwood as helpful to neighbors in need, as kind, and as religious "in his own way" (*TD*, August 12, 1984, p. D-2). He also noted that women were crazy about Linwood.

Indeed the Brileys as ladies' men seem typical of the traditional Badmen. Linwood and James have been described by some sources as handsome; all agree they were neat and meticulous in their dress. Linwood described his outfit on the night of the Barton Avenue murders: "I had a white hat on, a pair of suede and blue shoes, a pair of jeans and a blue suede shirt—I had suede to match my shoes."[3] Linwood, who was 5'9" tall and weighed between 150 and 170 pounds, and James, who was 6'3" tall and weighed about 180 pounds, were both very popular with women. Although neither was married at the time of his incarceration, both had an illegitimate child. Testimony at the trials indicates that girl friends frequently visited them at their home, spent time in their rooms, and even, according to their father, sometimes did their laundry.[4] None of Linwood's girlfriends had any negative comments to make about him when interviewed by the news media—despite the fact that each knew of his many other women. One suggested that his passion for cars offered her more competition than his affairs with other women (*TD*, August 12, 1984, p. D-2). Girl friends were conspicuously present during several of their trials, and several women offered testimony to refute the charges against the brothers. During Linwood's trial for the murders of Charles Garner and Blanche Page, one woman testified that she had met with a group belonging to a drug and prostitution ring that was planning the murders of Garner and Mrs. Page. During Linwood's trial for the murder of Harvey Wilkerson, Judy Barton, and their son Harvey, Linwood's and James's girlfriends testified that Linwood was at home at the time of the murders; indeed Linwood's girlfriend insisted the two of them were in his room lying down.[5]

Long Gone

During Linwood's trial for the murder of Mary Wilfong, his girlfriend testified that they were together elsewhere during the time that the murder occurred. Their girlfriends seemed to have faithfully visited them even after their incarceration, and three women attempted to smuggle guns to Linwood and Earl Clanton in Mecklenburg in October 1981. In his diary Dennis W. Stockton claimed that Linwood got him to write sexy love letters to a white pen pal (*Pilot*, September 16, 1984, p. C-11). Reverend Brown recalls that Linwood was indeed popular with the ladies: "He got proposals from women—women who knew him and women who didn't know him. Women would write him and send him their pictures." During their period of freedom in Philadelphia, Dan Latham, at whose garage they lived and worked, noted that their conversations frequently focused on women (*TD*, June 21, 1984), and the bounty hunter hired by the FBI to set them up for arrest recalled that one of their major topics of conversation was sex (*TD*, May 26, 1985, p. A-2). Fellow escapee Derick Peterson told me that James had met a woman in Philadelphia during their flight who wanted him to move into her New Jersey home with her (conversation, June 28, 1985). FBI Agent Carbonell recalls that following his arrest of James Briley, he said to him, "Boy, we really screwed up your night, didn't we?" and James boasted in terms that he could not quote to the effect that it did not make any difference because they had already, in the agent's genteel paraphrasing, "procured female companionship for that evening" (interview, June 25, 1985). On the day of James Briley's execution, a twenty-four-year-old woman from his neighborhood testified that she was a former girlfriend of Duncan Eric Meekins (the key witness whose testimony led to the conviction of the Brileys) and that Meekins had confessed to her that he committed the crimes for which James was being executed. A letter which she had written to James Briley was produced at the trial, and in the letter she had avowed that she would do anything to help save him, even if it meant her own prison sentence would be extended (she was at the time serving a five-year prison sentence for grand larceny).

The brothers' reported love of fine, fast cars also is reminiscent

The Men on the Loose

of the traditional Badmen's similar affinity. They reportedly spent a great deal of time tinkering with cars, and Linwood, at least, loved to drive fast. During his trial when he was asked about driving so fast when the detectives were trailing him, he responded, "I drive fast all the time . . . that's call normal driving to me."[6]

Neighbors also noted that the brothers spent their time helping neighbors in need (*TD*, August 12, 1984, p. D-2). The Brileys' consideration and generosity were also noted by Reverend Brown. He pointed out that they risked recognition in stopping and helping people fix flat tires during their trip to Philadelphia; and he also observed that Linwood consoled and inspired his visitors during his last days:

> "Linwood suggested to me that I not see the execution, because he realized that I had become emotionally involved with him and he saw my reactions—because when I would go to see him on the last couple of days, I just . . . [long pause] smoked HIS cigarettes."
>
> [Dance]: "He seems at this point like someone who was concerned about other people more than himself?"
>
> "ALL the time! ALL the time!"

Reverend Brown also found Linwood "a *very en-ga-ging* person," with a sense of humor:

> You could sit down and talk to him for HOURS! . . . He could make a joke out of anything. For example, when he was supposed to die [the first scheduled execution], they moved everybody from Death Row except Linwood. And Tuggle said he wasn't going anywhere. And Linwood found a great deal of joy in talking about Tuggle's resistance. He said, "Odie, you know, Tuggle kept saying, 'I ain't going. Yawl go have to take me [dramatizing his resistance].' " And if you could see Tuggle, then you would understand. And Linwood would demonstrate. And he say, "All the time they were picking him up and carrying him out and he saying, 'I ain't going nowhere!' "
>
> . . . .
>
> When I told him, I say [confidential tone, whispering], "Linwood, you know, I think they're *watching* me" (you know the folk

around the jail because I was going around just arguing with folk that this man shouldn't die because I think he's innocent). I say, "Linwood, you know, they *watching* me. I think they think I'm going *off*," and he say [also whispering in confidential tone], "Well, if they watching you, they should lock both of us up in here so they can watch both of us at the same time."

. . . .

One day I was down there eating with him. And I LIKE cantaloupe. They sent the cantaloupe already cut up. I got down there at the time he was eating cantaloupe. And he said—he would NEVER eat without offering you some—and he say, "You have some cantaloupe?" And I said, "Man, I love cantaloupe." And he was in the cell and I was outside the cell sitting in a chair. And I'm reaching my hand through the cell and eating this cantaloupe. He say, "What would your members say if they saw you eating cantaloupe with the mass killer, Linwood Briley!" He could laugh; he could joke about it. And this led me to believe that this boy is not a mass killer.

Neighbors of the Brileys also noted that the brothers maintained close family ties (*TD*, August 12, 1984, p. D-2), a fact frequently evident throughout their ordeal. The mother, father, brothers, uncles, and aunts quietly supported the two condemned members of their family until the end. One uncle even was arrested with them when they were recaptured in Philadelphia after the Great Escape and was charged with assisting them during their escape (the charges were dropped). An aunt testified in Linwood's trial for the murders of Page and Garner that he was in North Carolina at the time. Their father was with Linwood when he was picked up for the crimes for which he was executed and was later charged with perjuring himself during one of the trials. Although some friends allege that problems with the sons contributed to the separation of the parents, no rumors of any family rifts associated with the numerous long-time legal conflicts and complications in which the brothers were involved ever publicly surfaced. The family members did not parade the agony nor the angst they obviously experienced during this time. They simply quietly did what they could to support and offer their love to their sons/brothers/nephews/etc.

The Men on the Loose

The newest member of the family was no less ardent in her support but much more outspoken. Evangeline G. Redding, who married James Briley forty-nine days before his execution, managed from the moment of the engagement to be almost constantly in the public eye. She believed that the failure of the brothers to grant media interviews prevented the public from having any real vision of them to counteract the portrayal of them as monsters that was propagated by the media.

The closeness of the three brothers prosecuted for the series of murders in Richmond again is notable. As they went through endless trials for murder, rape, robbery, and lesser crimes, neither one ever turned on the other or in any way compromised the other to save or protect himself. Throughout their imprisonment, they apparently supported and sustained one another. Despite their powerlessness as prisoners, they fought to remain together. When Linwood and James Briley were returned to the State Penitentiary following their escape, their brother Anthony, referred to as Bebe (pronounced bā-bā) by his friends, was moved to the State Farm, where he was at first put in isolation, though, according to inmate friends, he himself had done nothing. According to the prison grapevine when he was offered his freedom to return to the general prison population, he refused and continued in isolation as a form of protest (conversation, Virginia State Penitentiary, November 26, 1984). When James Briley was to be taken away from the Virginia State Penitentiary (where all of the escapees had been returned following their escape), he refused to leave his brother Linwood, whose execution date was fast approaching. This information, which was conveyed to me during a conversation at the Virginia State Penitentiary on August 6, 1984, was substantiated by James Briley in his press conference on April 16, 1985: "I told them I wouldn't leave my brother. I wouldn't walk out." And James Briley couldn't be dragged out until he had been shot *twice* with a stun gun. Before the time of the executions, family members spent as much time as possible with the two condemned brothers, and the imprisoned brothers held lengthy telephone conversations with one another. Following Linwood's execution, James wrote an elegy to his brother, in which he praised him as a man who was "sweet," who stood "fast & strong," who was a victim of a "Political wrong," and who was misrepresented as "A Mad-man—a monster" by "people who knew him not at all." The poem details his refusal to leave his brother, their last telephone conversation during which his brother expressed his love for him, and Linwood's execution, and then concludes with the assurance that his brother is in heaven. The poem, which was published in the *FYSK Magazine* (13 [Winter 1984], 18) is signed "Beloved Brother . . . . . . James Briley" and dated October 12, 1984.

I never met Linwood Briley, but I did have a conversation with James Briley at Mecklenburg Correctional Center's Death Row on February 28, 1985. When I first walked into the area outside the day room, I was shocked by the sense that I had of the inmates on Death Row as caged animals, rushing to the bars to chatter to and view the visitors. It seemed a painfully dehumanizing situation, no matter which side of the bars one stood on. It was not at all that there was anything animal-like about the behavior of the men—indeed, given their circumstances, those with whom I spoke stood tall and spoke with some command and at times with great intelligence. Nor had they regressed to the distant, blank, expressionless, morose nonpersons devoid of a sense of individuality described by Rollo May in "The Man Who Was Put in a Cage." But their situation was one that at first overwhelmed the visitor with a feeling of great despair and pity. Oddly enough, when James Briley appeared, some minutes after my arrival, he had such a dominating presence that he dispelled this mood for me and allowed me to enjoy my conversation with him almost unmindful of the bars and the general ambience. He was very neatly dressed in his prison garb, which, like the cell bars, seemed not to detract from his rather lofty bearing. There appeared to be an immediate deference to him by the other prisoners, since it seemed that no one else talked while he spoke with me. (I'm not positive that my impression here is correct—it may simply be that I was oblivious to the chatter that seemed to dominate before he appeared). He impressed me during our talk as pleasant, confident, intelligent, eloquent, friendly, soft-spoken, but pow-

The Men on the Loose

erful and fully in control. He seemed to accept the deference of others as his due and to acknowledge with a small, knowing, wry smile indications of the responses of others to him. He revealed a sense of humor and he smiled and laughed easily—but not loudly or even unrestrainedly. He was optimistic about a new lawyer (JoAnne Little's lawyer, he told me) and a new friend (who was shortly to become his wife). We chatted about mutual acquaintances and basically enjoyed a comfortable unrestrained conversation that belied the reality of the fact that I was standing on Death Row and enjoying a pleasant tête-à-tête with a man who had been implicated in some of the most vicious crimes Richmond had ever known. The James Briley I was talking to seemed an absolute contradiction to the infamous perpetrator of those horrendous acts and to the James Briley that some other people recalled.

Some neighbors recall that the Briley boys (the references were generally to James, Linwood, and Anthony, I believe, though people tend not to make individual distinctions and to speak in general terms of "the Briley brothers" or "the Briley boys") were discipline problems all through their adolescence, and that they were too often defended by at least one overly protective parent. One neighbor charged that they were not properly disciplined or supervised as youngsters, and detailed a long list of vandalisms and pranks of which they were accused, including throwing eggs and trash on cars and at houses. Several people alleged that they played with guns; one joked that they had completely wiped out all the birds and other animals in the area.[7] One family in the neighborhood is convinced that a shot through their living room door around the time that a neighbor was killed by Linwood Briley, who claimed to be shooting at birds, was caused by one of them. Their choice of pets (they reportedly had a boa constrictor, a tarantula, piranhas, and what was frequently described [in a clear exaggeration] as "a pack of dogs") impressed many people as suggestive of their viciousness.[8]

Other people in the area had such fear of the Brileys that they would not dream of saying anything about them. Once when I was inquiring in the area about the Brileys, a friend explained to me that the mere fact that the Briley brothers were on Death Row did not mean that these people were protected from their vengeance. He and they felt that the brothers had the contacts and the influence and the power to retaliate, despite the fact that they were incarcerated. The obvious terror in the eyes of some of these people upon the mention of the Briley brothers was so grave as to discourage any further inquiries. I thus was unable to determine the degree to which their fears might have stemmed from some actual acquaintance with the Brileys or from an awareness of the crimes of which they were accused from the media.

One source suggested that even when the brothers were in elementary and middle school, they were very threatening and aroused unusual fear in both students and teachers. Several former teachers and classmates from middle and high school recalled that the brothers created problems in school and were guilty of a number of pranks and more serious infractions. They were frequently called into the principals' offices and several times suspended, their final suspension being related to legal difficulties. They were both poor students, a result, according to some teachers, of their frequent failure to attend class and their indifference. Teachers in both middle school and high school noted that their mother was a very concerned parent who regularly called the teachers and came to the schools for conferences regarding the problems her sons were experiencing.

I did not hear many negative comments about the Briley brothers from inmates. As previously noted, several prisoners who knew them from the streets and from prison had very positive responses to them. One must, however, consider the possibility that inmates who may have had different reactions may well have been afraid to voice them for fear of retaliation. One former inmate (white) was quoted in the *News Leader* (October 13, 1984) as saying that he despised Linwood Briley whom he knew in prison, and who "came in saying, 'I'm Linwood Briley and I killed eight people. I'm bad.' He tended to play the bad [guy]." He insisted that Linwood Briley was regarded by other convicts as "the sleaze at the bottom of the barrel." Another white inmate at Mecklenburg commented, "I feel the Brileys were animals. The

The Men on the Loose

crimes that they committed were so hideous and coldblooded!" (June 1985). Some Black prisoners were also appalled at the nature of their crimes, especially their murder of a pregnant woman and a child, an atrocity that has become even more gruesome in the accounts commonly circulating at Mecklenburg, where several inmates mistakenly believed that the fetus was cut out of the mother's stomach and that the young son was forced to witness the rape and butchering of his mother (June 1985 and August 15, 1985).[9] The fact is that the mother was raped in the kitchen while the son was held in the living room (telephone interview, Sgt. Norman Harding, August 20, 1985).

Linwood Briley, who was thirty years old at the time of his escape, had been on Mecklenburg's Death Row since January 28, 1980. He was implicated in a series of crimes, beginning in 1969 when he was tried as a juvenile and given a suspended sentence for a break-in and snatching a purse.

In 1970, when he was sixteen, he was again tried as a juvenile for involuntary manslaughter in the death of a neighbor who lived on the street behind him. The body of the elderly woman was found in her yard, and it was assumed that she had suffered a heart attack brought on by the death of her husband, from whose funeral she had just returned. It was not until later that funeral directors noticed that she had been shot and an investigation led to Linwood Briley. Briley contended that he was shooting at birds and that he had no idea that he was responsible for the neighbor's death until police came for him (interview with Sgt. Norman Harding, Richmond, June 5, 1985).[10] Briley was found "not innocent" of the charges and sent to Beaumont Learning Center in February 1971, where he remained until March 1972. According to psychological reports prepared at the time, Linwood showed no remorse for the killing but rather noted that "she would have died anyhow, for he had heard from someone that she had heart trouble" (*TD*, August 12, 1984, p. D-2).[11]

In April 1974 Linwood Briley was sentenced to seven years in prison, with four years suspended, for two charges of breaking and entering. He was sent to Southampton Correctional Center, from which he was released in 1976.

Long Gone

In 1976 he was charged with felonious assault and robbery, but he was acquitted of those charges; a few years later, however, when his room was searched in connection with other charges, a watch stolen from the victim of that 1976 crime was found (*NL*, July 6, 1984, p. 14).

Testimony offered by Duncan Meekins—a teen-age friend—information obtained by police in their investigation, and evidence from other sources implicated Linwood Briley in a string of vicious crimes committed in the Richmond area between March and October 1979.[12]

The reign of terror apparently began on March 12, 1979, when Linwood went to the Henrico County home of William and Virginia Bucher and asked to use the telephone because his car had broken down. When he was allowed to enter the home, he pulled a gun and admitted his brother Anthony. They tied up the Buchers, ransacked their home, sprayed flammable liquid all around, and set the house on fire. Bucher was able to free himself and his wife and escape the fire. The police scanner seized by police in their search of the Briley house on October 24 of that year was determined by police to be the one stolen from the Bucher home (interview, Sgt. Harding).

On March 21, 1979, Michael W. McDuffe was shot to death in Henrico County. Allegedly Linwood and Anthony Briley, aware that he was carrying a large amount of cash, robbed him and drove off with him in his own car; Linwood shot their victim as Anthony drove the car, and they abandoned the car and corpse in eastern Henrico County. No charges were brought in that case.

On March 31, 1979, Linwood Briley and Duncan Meekins allegedly went to the East End home of Edric Alvin Clark, twenty-eight, to get drugs. An argument ensued, and Clark was shot with a rifle. This case was not prosecuted.

On April 9, 1979, Mary W. Gowen, seventy-six, of Richmond, was reportedly followed by Meekins and Linwood and Anthony Briley as she left a North Side home where she had been babysitting and went to her West End apartment. Outside the apartment building, she was robbed, raped, and fatally shot. No charges were brought in this case.

The Men on the Loose

On July 4, 1979, Linwood and Anthony Briley and Meekins were reportedly casing some houses on Seminary Avenue, when they discovered Christopher M. Phillips, seventeen, tampering with Linwood's car. When they questioned him and he claimed the car belonged to a friend of his, an argument ensued, and they began to beat him. Another boy who was with Phillips fled, and the gang took Phillips in the back yard of a house off Seminary Avenue where Linwood allegedly hit him in the head with a cinderblock, killing him. No charges were brought in this case.

On September 14, 1979, according to the testimony of Meekins, the Brileys abducted Richmond disc jockey John "Johnny G from Tennessee" Gallagher, fifty-one, from the parking lot of a South Side Richmond nightclub. They took his wallet, which netted them $30.00, according to Meekins,[13] a watch and a couple of rings, forced Gallaher into his car, drove around, finally taking him to Mayo's Island, where Linwood Briley shot him in the back with a rifle. Linwood Briley was sentenced to death for this crime.

On September 30, 1979, the gang followed Mary S. Wilfong, a sixty-two-year-old private nurse, as she left the North Side area, watched as she dropped off a passenger, and then continued to tail her to her Western Henrico apartment, near Willow Lawn. James Briley, who broke her skull with a baseball bat and took her pocketbook, was convicted of murder and robbery for this crime and sentenced to twenty years for each charge; Linwood Briley was convicted of capital murder and robbery, for which he was sentenced to life plus fifty years.

On October 6, 1979, the Briley brothers and Meekins went to the home of Blanche Page, in the same block on Fifth Avenue as the Brileys' Fourth Avenue home. They offered to sell stolen citizens band radios to Mrs. Page, a seventy-five-year-old invalid, and Charles Garner, fifty-nine, a boarder at her home. Police suspect that Mr. Garner might have had some contact with the Brileys prior to this date (interview, Sgt. Harding), but they are sure Mrs. Page did not know them. The Brileys and Meekins were admitted into the house, whereupon they beat Mrs. Page to death with a pipe and bludgeoned and stabbed Mr. Garner. His body was found with four butcher knives, a carving fork, and one blade of a pair of scissors stuck in his back (most newspaper accounts of this crime indicate that there were three knives or six knives, but Sgt. Harding checked his report of the crime the day before our interview and assured me that the correct number was four). When I questioned Sgt. Harding's assertion that the knives had been plunged *all* the way in the victim's back so that it was impossible to check for fingerprints, he reiterated "Yeah, but those knives had been pushed *all* the way down into his back and there was just no way of getting a fingerprint off—it was that much sticking out from the back [indicating about an inch]. This is what you call overkill." After Garner was killed, a fire was started on his back, the curtains on the kitchen door were set on fire, and papers on the kitchen cabinet were ignited. Linwood Briley received a life sentence for Garner's murder and fifty years for Mrs. Page's murder as well as twenty years for robbery and one year for the use of a firearm in the commission of a robbery.

On October 14, 1979, Thomas Saunders, a thirty-two-year-old Vietnam veteran, was involved in a fight with Linwood and James Briley and Meekins. Reportedly, one of the Brileys threw a gun to Meekins, who fatally wounded the East End resident. No charges were brought in this case.

Other cases that the Richmond police were investigating and in which they believe the Brileys were involved included the rape of an older white woman on Laburnum Avenue. Her husband was hit in the head with a baseball bat, but neither was killed. No charges were brought in this case. In another instance a woman was followed down a North Side street; when she saw a group of men coming after her, she threw her pocketbook down and ran. They caught up with her on somebody else's porch and shot a 45 that was connected with at least four other cases, but the shot went over her head and she was not injured (interview, Harding). A South Side resident was reportedly grabbed by Linwood and Meekins, who attempted to rob him. One shot fired at him missed; then the gun jammed. By this time neighbors began to look out of their windows, and the attackers fled (*TD*, October 13, 1984, p. A-8).

For some months prior to October 1979, Richmond police had

The Men on the Loose

received reports from informants that Linwood Briley and others were committing robberies in the Richmond area. When they received additional tips that October, Richmond police assigned two detectives to join the Special Actions Force of Henrico County, which was also investigating Linwood Briley, to maintain surveillance of the suspect. This group of detectives trailed Linwood Briley and three other males, whose identity they did not then know, to Barton Avenue on the night of October 19. They did not see where their subjects went, but they waited for them.

James, Linwood, and Anthony Briley and Duncan Meekins, while drinking alcohol and smoking marijuana at the Briley home earlier in the evening, had decided to go to rob Harvey Wilkerson, twenty-six, who had grown up in the same neighborhood as the Brileys. First James and Linwood, and then Anthony and Meekins entered the Barton Avenue apartment where Wilkerson lived with Judy Barton, twenty-three, and their son, Harvey, and, according to one version given by Meekins, visited for a while. Then they forced their unsuspecting hosts to lie on the floor, binding and gagging the adults. (At the trials Meekins testified that when he and Anthony went into the apartment, the adults had already been tied up.) At some point during the incident a choker chain, the type used to restrain dogs, was placed around the child's neck. While they ransacked the house, Linwood, James, and Meekins took turns raping Judy Barton, who was three-months pregnant. Then James Briley reportedly shot Ms. Barton in the head and commanded Meekins, "You got to get one too," whereupon Meekins shot Wilkerson in the head.[14] James Briley shot their five-year-old son Harvey in the head just prior to leaving.

Police outside heard shots and called headquarters to ask if any reports of shooting had been made. None had been received. They later observed the Brileys and Meekins returning to their car with a rifle and a grocery bag; they observed Meekins drop the rifle and stoop to pick it up; one detective thought he saw James stick a pistol down in his pants.[15] They sped away in Linwood's car with the lights off, and the detectives set off in hot pursuit. The gang eluded police and threw the rifle away. Later the police caught up with them and followed them to the Briley

The bodies of Wilkerson, Barton, and little Harvey were not discovered until two days later. It was a ghastly scene. The adults had been covered with sheets. Two boa constrictors and two doberman pinschers roamed freely through the house. "The dogs inside had eaten [the child's] ear off and eaten into the wound on his face.. . . And the dogs had been walking around in the blood and it was feces all over the floor" (interview, Harding).

The day after the discovery of the bodies, police, who had had Linwood Briley under surveillance, had seen the four men in the area of the crime, had heard gunshots, and had seen them leaving with a gun, took out a warrant for Linwood's arrest. They sent some twenty units over in the North Side area in different rotations watching for him. Then at around 7 P.M. on October 22, 1979, they spotted his car. Linwood was driving, Meekins was in the passenger side, and James Briley, Sr., the father, was in the back seat. Linwood was arrested, and he and Meekins were taken into custody. Sgt. Harding drove Linwood's car to police headquarters: "On the day of the arrest of Linwood Briley, I personally drove his maroon Nova down to police headquarters. And I had left my police radio in my unit, which was driven back to police headquarters by another detective. As I was driving down the street, I heard police calls coming in on a radio, and I happened to raise up the seat rest on the right, and I found a police scanner" (Harding). He realized that Linwood, possessed of a scanner later determined to have been stolen from the Bucher family, had been privy to the communications of the police as they had been following him during the days preceding his arrest, a fact that was clearly confirmed during the trials.

When Meekins was picked up, Sgt. Harding called his parents in before questioning him because he was a juvenile, only sixteen years old. Within about an hour, Meekins had begun his confession: "What I convinced him to talk to us about, I say, 'You can lie to me all you want to, but don't lie to your parents who raised you.' So he asked them, 'You want me to tell the truth?' and his parents told him, 'Yeah, tell the truth' " (Harding). Meekins' attorney agreed to let him provide information provided he did

The Men on the Loose

not receive the death penalty and did not get any more time than the Brileys. Information which Meekins provided to Richmond and Henrico police was the major factor in the implication of the Brileys in the string of crimes that had terrorized the Richmond and Henrico communities since March.

Meekins, who lived two doors from the Brileys on Fourth Avenue, was a close friend of Anthony's. Although he implicated Anthony in the string of crimes, he never accused him of committing any of the murders; Sgt. Harding observed that "In the testimony it seemed like Duncan Meekins was trying to kind of look out for Anthony Briley." At one point in the trial of James Dyral Briley for the Barton Avenue murders, Meekins was asked if he saw Anthony with a gun, and he responded, "I ain't never seen him with one."[16]

Having received a death sentence, four life sentences for murder, rape, and robbery, and miscellaneous other shorter sentences for robbery and the use of a firearm in the commission of a felony, Linwood Briley was incarcerated at Mecklenburg Correctional Center on January 28, 1980. With the exception of the nineteen days that he was a fugitive from the Mecklenburg Correctional Center, he spent the remainder of his life in prison, from his arrest on October 22, 1979, to his execution on October 12, 1984, at the age of thirty.

James Briley, who was twenty-seven years old at the time of his flight from Mecklenburg (he celebrated his twenty-eighth birthday during his escape), joined his brother at Mecklenburg's Death Row on March 4, 1980. He was implicated in a series of crimes beginning when he was a teenager. When he was sixteen he was involved in a robbery and shootout with the law, in which he was shot. At his trial for that offense in 1973, when he was seventeen, he was found guilty of robbery and attempted murder and sentenced to twenty years in prison. James Briley admitted that crime: "I made some mistakes in my earlier days. . . . I armed robbed a store, shot at a police officer. I made a mistake and I went to prison" (press conference, Virginia State Penitentiary, April 16, 1985). James Briley was released on parole on September 3, 1979,[17] at which time he allegedly joined his brothers and

Meekins in their crime spree, including the murders of Gallaher, Wilfong, Saunders, and the Harvey Wilkerson family.

On the afternoon of October 19, 1979, James Briley appeared before Richmond Judge Frank A.S. Wright, who admonished him to abide by the terms of his parole. According to his parole officer, James assured the judge that he "had no plans of getting . . . involved in any trouble; that he was going to do what he could to stay off the street."[18] That night the Wilkerson family was killed. Three days later on October 22 James Briley was arrested when he and Anthony went down to police headquarters to check on Linwood, who had been picked up earlier that evening. Sentenced to death for capital murder during robbery and for capital murder during rape (in the deaths of Judy Barton and her son Harvey), to life for five counts of first degree murder, and to miscellaneous other terms for other crimes such as robbery and the use of a firearm in a felony, James Briley was sent to Mecklenburg on March 4, 1980. When he was electrocuted on April 18, 1985, at the age of twenty-eight, he had spent all of his life since his original incarceration at seventeen, except 68 days (including the 19 days of his flight from Mecklenburg), in various Virginia prisons.

During their arrests, their interrogations, and their lengthy trials the Briley brothers were constantly noted as being calm and composed. Upon their arrests they denied involvement and remained "very calm and collected" (Harding). At the trial, the neatly dressed defendants sat quietly, often taking notes. They sometimes took the stand in their own defense, offering alibis for their whereabouts at the time of the murders and providing explanations to contradict the overwhelming evidence being presented against them. Throughout their arrests, initial interrogations, trials, appeals, and interviews, they persistently maintained their innocence. They did not, however, seem to publicly express hostility toward the system which they maintained unfairly convicted them.[19] When I asked Reverend Brown, who was with Linwood daily until his death, if he ever revealed anger or hostility, he replied, "Never did!" Indeed Reverend Brown paused and pondered aloud: "Could you say he was unemotional? I never saw him manifest any type of outward emotions—except . . . calmness. EVEN up until the last."

On March 28, 1985, James Briley married Evangeline G. Redding, a freelance writer who had approached him about writing a book about him. Her concern for his imprisonment and for the plight of Black men who have been victimized by the justice system impressed him, he related in his April 16, 1985, press conference. She found it difficult to obtain visiting privileges because she was not a member of his family, and thus suggested to him that they marry. He agreed, they fell in love (they both maintained), and they married, the first wedding to be held at the Virginia State Penitentiary's Death Row.[20]

Jet described the marriage ceremony as being set "in the bowels of the prison, cockroaches scurrying by" and noted that the bride gave Briley a set of boudoir photographs since conjugal visits are prohibited at the prison (April 22, 1985, p. 12). The new Mrs. Briley insisted that their marriage would give her "credibility to fight for him" (*NL*, March 20, 1985, p. 1), and she immediately set out to call media attention to her husband and his plight. She arranged a press conference with his family and attacked his volunteer lawyers for being ineffective and preventing the public from viewing his human side by keeping him from the news media. She accused the lawyers of ordering him to keep quiet "like a good little boy" (*NL*, April 17, 1985, p. 11) and proceeded to hire a New York lawyer. She was interviewed by *Jet* Magazine (April 22, 1985 issue, pp. 12-14). James himself held a press conference on April 16, 1985, the first time that he had granted any interviews during the whole ordeal. She was very much in evidence during the period immediately preceding the execution, demonstrating in front of the State Penitentiary and finally riding away from the prison after her last visit with her husband on the day of his execution.

CHAPTER 4

On the Road
to Freedom

Itinerary of the Travelers

I'm free, I'm free, I'm free at last.
Thank God Almighty, I'm free at last.

Traditional

Oh, freedom, Oh, freedom, Oh, freedom over me.

Traditional

When they reached the other shore . . .
They sang a song of triumph o'er . . .

"Go Down Moses," Traditional

At 10:47 P.M. on May 31, 1984, the six condemned men from Mecklenburg's Death Row pulled their white van out onto Route 58, which runs by the Mecklenburg Correctional Center, and then traveled south on Route 4, an old, winding, little traveled country road, heading for North Carolina, $783 richer with money which they allegedly took from their captives (*NL*, June 5, 1984, p. 4).[1] They drove at a normal speed, Tuggle estimates between 60 and 70 mph. They did not want to risk being stopped for speeding (Lem Tuggle, Richmond, July 8, 1985). As they drove away they clapped and cheered and prayed. They felt happy, joyous, free! It was too early to absorb the reality that they were actually out: Lem Tuggle recalls, "We all started to cheering and hollering, 'We made it, we're free!' We said we couldn't believe that they had actually let us out like that" (June 28, 1985). Derick Peterson notes, "[When we first got out] all of us were in our own thoughts. I was TOLD that something happened, but I was like blanked out right. Really, I was just enjoying the scenery, right, being out for the first time in, what, two years. It was like, you know, EVERY-THING was beautiful to me, right, the road and everything else, o.k. It was wonderful, just being out" (June 28, 1985). It was indeed a scenic back road that they had taken, mostly woods, corn and tobacco fields, and an occasional country store advertising fishing bait. It led across the John H. Kerr Dam. The Brileys must have also felt the elation of experiencing freedom again. Eighteen months before the escape they had written letters to school children in which they asserted, "You can take our word for it, you don't know how precious your freedom is until you've lost it" (*Commonwealth Times*, November 20- December3, 1984, p. 3).

The men debated what their next move should be. They decided that they should head for "the closest place we could get that would be out of state" (Tuggle, June 28, 1985), and that they should get rid of the van as soon as possible and find some other means of transportation. They considered many possibilities, even ramming another vehicle on the highway and then taking it over when the driver stopped. They crossed the North Carolina border in a matter of minutes and drove on to the end of Route 4, turned left onto Route 1, passing "Soul City," and continued into the small town of Warrenton, about forty miles from the Mecklenburg Correctional Center. There they drove past the side of the Marian Boyd School (which is on Cousin Lacy's Lane) and abandoned the van at the end of that dead-end street behind the school.

Although the Brileys had needed the others to pull off the escape, they seemed eager to ditch them, investigators told me. Agents assume, however, that Tuggle and Jones, not knowing what to do, "just tagged along behind the Brileys" (interview, anonymity requested, June 1985). Peterson, not inclined to follow along behind others, was the first one to leave the group and set out on his own, heading toward town: "Clanton, he followed behind me—well, it won't like he *followed* behind me, but he just came in the general direction where I was going—that's how we got together" (Peterson, June 28, 1985). Thus, despite their initial plans to separate once they got out of Mecklenburg, the escapees

Long Gone

was likewise unplanned. "It just sort of worked out that way" (Tuggle, June 28, 1985).

About 12:30 A.M. on June 1 two men, originally believed to be the Brileys, jumped into the car of Andrew Davis when he stopped at a red light on Main Street (one block from the Marian Boyd School) in Warrenton, North Carolina. When they yelled to him, he at first thought it might have been someone he knew. They then leaped into the car and inquired about where they could find drugs and some action, and Davis informed them that Warrenton (with a population of 1,063) did not have drugs and "folds up the sidewalks" about 10 P.M. (*NL*, June 2, 1984, p. 5). After driving for about ten minutes, he became suspicious and stopped the car, whereupon one of the men placed a knife to his throat. The terrified driver screamed and the convicts dropped their knife in his car and fled. The victim as well as the investigators were at first quite confident that the assailants were the Brileys. On July 12, 1984, Robert M. Landon, then director of the Virginia Department of Corrections, told me that despite the countless unsubstantiated reports of incidents involving the Brileys, "We're pretty sure of that one" (July 12, 1984). During the early days of the escape, one spokesman for the Department of Corrections lamented, "Everybody is Linwood Briley" (*NL*, June 6, 1984). Later developments in their inquiry, however, led investigators to believe that it was Peterson and Clanton who commandeered that car (interview, anonymity requested, June 1985), a suspicion confirmed in my conversation with Peterson. I asked Peterson why they ran instead of taking the car and if they panicked. He laughed and noted, "We didn't want to hurt nobody, right, and this individual who the car belonged to was so hyped up, it was either hurt him and get the car or just leave him alone, you understand, and so we just left him alone. Like I said, we didn't want to hurt nobody."

Unable to secure a car, Peterson and Clanton spent the night in a well-concealed spot in the woods. Their searchers came *very* close: "They got so close to us, so close, like I could hear the dogs, I could see the flashlights, I could hear the folks talking. All of a

Grateful acknowledgment is made to Richmond Newspapers, Inc., for permission to use the above cartoon by Gary Brookins. Cartoon appeared in the *Times-Dispatch* on June 20, 1984.

sudden they start fading away. I say, is this all they gon do? If **65**
they come in here, man, we gone. Cause I'm thinking now, I say,
shit, they go shoot us, no doubt, we out here in this woods all by
ourselves, man, ain't nobody to say nothing. They might even
plant a couple a guns on us. Cause they had already said we was
armed and dangerous."

Meanwhile, the Brileys, Tuggle, and Jones continued up Main
Street, looking for a car to steal. Tuggle and Linwood rode stolen
bicycles (one twenty-inch bike and one English three-speed)
during this quest, while James Briley and Jones kept up on foot
(interview with investigator, June, 1985, and conversation with
Tuggle, June 28, 1985). It must have been one hilarious scene, one
FBI agent suggested to me, and Tuggle chuckled as he recalled
the episode. Tuggle, the largest of the group, was riding the
twenty-inch bike and his knees kept banging against the handle
bars. He wasn't moving as fast on the bicycle as those on foot.
Finally they threw the bikes down by the side of the road and
continued on foot. They were going from house to house, looking
for a car. When they first started out, big comfortable homes lined
both sides of Main Street, but as they continued their trek up
Route 401 (Main Street) the houses were widely scattered. After
traveling a little over four miles, at about 3 A.M. they came to
Paynter's Welding Shop, where they discovered a Ford Ranger
pickup truck with the keys left in the ignition near the Warren
community of Afton. They filled the gas tank and headed north.
They took Route 85 to 95, drove through Richmond on Route 95,
going through the Belvidere toll booth (just north of the down-
town area and the exit for the Virginia State Penitentiary, this toll
booth is only a couple of miles from the Brileys' home). By daybreak they were already north of Richmond, where they stopped
to refuel and to eat in a fast food restaurant. Tuggle recalls taking
off his guard's uniform in this area (all of the men had on their
prison garb—blue jeans or sweat shirts under their guards' uniforms), and the rest of them removed their uniforms somewhere
north of Richmond. They continued north, gassing up again in
Thornburg (interview, Landon, July 12, 1984), and driving on up
the Delaware Turnpike. Tuggle, who reportedly had marijuana

On the Road to Freedom

with him during the trip that he had obtained while on Death Row (*TD*, July 6, 1984), as did the Brileys (*TD*, May 26, 1985, p. A-2), was later to acclaim that they "partied all the way up the East Coast" (*TD*, June 10, 1984, p. A-2). Some rumors suggested that the three Black escapees rode in the truck and forced Tuggle to ride on the back, but one agent told me that they thought all four men squeezed into the cab of the truck, a theory confirmed by Tuggle: "It was pretty crowded, but we all sat in the front" (June 28, 1985).

In the meantime the next day Peterson and Clanton removed their guards' uniforms (Peterson had on a sweat suit and Clanton had on sweat pants, a T-shirt, and a guard's jacket with the patches taken off [conversation, Peterson, June 28, 1985]) and jogged down Hall Street into town to buy some groceries to take back to their hideaway. They went to Willoughby's Convenience Store and Laundromat on Macon Street in Warrenton. Clanton made a telephone call, and Peterson reportedly tried to call his mother, though he told me he made no calls. They bought some wine, cigarettes, bread and cheese in the store and went into the adjoining laundromat. People in Warrenton recall that they were nice and friendly and that they chatted with some people in the busy laundromat, even helped one woman carry her laundry out to her car (Warrenton, August 16, 1985). They then sat down in the laundromat to relax and, according to several reports, enjoy their cheese and wine.

The Brileys, Jones, and Tuggle continued driving north, stopping occasionally to help motorists in distress, according to Tuggle's contention later. When they got to Philadelphia, the Brileys stopped and bought some clothes and abandoned their guards' uniforms in a park, where they said goodbye to their cohorts after giving them $25.00 (*TD*, May 26, 1985, p. A-2). Tuggle continued the northward journey in the stolen vehicle with Jones: "I let Jones come along because he didn't have anyplace to go; the Brileys wouldn't let him go with them" (July 8, 1985). According to Tuggle, he stopped to help people in trouble—he helped one woman whose car battery was dead—he stopped to ask directions of a New Jersey state trooper, he stopped to buy scotch and to eat at fast-food restaurants. He and Jones camped for two or three days near Woodford, Vermont, and then drove north to Jay, a small community ten miles south of the Canadian border, where they camped again, using a tent that Tuggle had found for shelter. Their days of freedom were recalled by Tuggle as "a dream come true" (*TD*, July 10, 1984, p. 1). Their pleasant, leisurely trip was marred somewhat by a lack of funds. Having exhausted the money given them by the Brileys and $17.00 that they had gotten in a sale of some of the spare parts of their stolen truck, Tuggle headed back south on June 8 to get some money to finance their trip to Canada, leaving Jones near the border. Tuggle's goal was to go "to Canada, where there was nobody living and just build a cabin . . . and just stay there the next 20 or 30 years. . . . What I was planning on doing was trapping, tanning hides and selling 'em" (*TD*, July 10, 1984, p. 1). He hoped to find some work, but when he got to Woodford he was running out of gasoline.

> "Lord, I'm broke and hungry,
> I ain't got a dime;
> Lord, I'm broke and hungry,
> I ain't got a dime."
>
> Traditional

In the meantime Jones broke into a house in Jay and called his mother in Richmond, Virginia. She tried to convince him to surrender.

> "My first stop was in Philly: I took the town by surprise. I pulled off a couple of pretty stings and laid low to avoid the eyes."
>
> "Sugar Hill," *The Life*, p. 93

Meanwhile the Brileys were in Philadelphia, living in a garage owned by Dan Latham.

> I'm goin' where nobody knows my name,
> Lawd, Lawd, Lawd, Lawd!
> I'm goin' where nobody knows my name.
>
> Traditional

The two brothers' uncle, Johnnie Lee Council, who lived near the park where Tuggle and Jones had separated from the Brileys, had

On the Road to Freedom

allegedly introduced them to Latham, who believed that they were Lucky (Linwood) and Slim (James), two drifters from Georgia. Latham and his neighbors found the two young men to be nice, quiet, hard-working young men, and Latham was delighted to have them help him prepare for the opening of his car repair shop.

> I stayed in a beat-up. . . house, the poorest of the low,
> But where all the hippest people stayed when they didn't
>   want to get caught.
>
> "Sugar Hill," *The Hill*, p. 93

Latham's garage, where Slim and Lucky lived, was in one of the most depressed and dangerous slum areas of Philadelphia, one which was described by a taxi driver as a section "where people live to prey on other people" (*TD*, June 21, 1984, p. 1). The neighborhood was so bad that the FBI agents who were tracking them were eager to get out as quickly as possible; Michael Carbonell, the agent who directed the search, told me they didn't spend much time looking for weapons after capturing the fugitives because "It's not the kind of place you want to hang around; we wanted to get out quickly because a large crowd had formed" (June 25, 1985). Not only did Slim and Lucky build things for the new shop, they cleaned, washed cars, did miscellaneous tasks, and served as watchmen for the garage. That it was helpful to have live-in guards in this kind of area was reinforced by the fact that the morning after their departure, Latham's garage was broken into and approximately $5,000 worth of tools stolen. The only pay Latham provided for the services of Slim and Lucky was permission to live in the garage and an occasional meal. They were big eaters, but they didn't drink hard liquor; they preferred pink champagne.

While they were in Philadelphia, Linwood allegedly spent a great deal of time searching for a person who he believed could help clear them of murder charges. He later told Reverend Odie Brown, "If I could get out of jail and clear my name, I would come back and willingly die in the electric chair" (interview with Reverend Brown, Richmond, June 17, 1985). Reverend Brown is con-

Long Gone

vinced that Linwood knew a man who could clear him: "I think [in this escape] he had something he wanted to prove; I think he wanted to clear the Briley name."[2] Investigators with whom I spoke, however, gave little credence to the theory that Linwood Briley was traveling around looking for someone who could clear him. According to Carbonell, Linwood had told the garage owner that he was learning his way around Philadelphia and looking for a job; he believes Linwood was moving around freely because he was feeling that everything was "cool" and did not feel the pressures of any close, heated pursuit.

Conversations with other inmates back at the Virginia State Penitentiary following their capture suggested that they had a great time during their freedom. Peterson told me, "You know they had been locked up for the last five or six years. They enjoyed everything that was happening, you know, videos and roller skating, and movies, and, you know, just LIFE, right. Just being out there. They did it up right, they did a lot of things—maybe that they shouldn't have done. They enjoyed themselves. I'm glad they did." He went on to say that James met a woman in Philadelphia from New Jersey who had asked him to come up and live with her. She was with him the day he was captured: "On the same night that they got jammed, they had been out all night. He said she was really shocked when she discovered who he was, that he was a Death Row escapee."

While they were living at the garage, they were befriended by Skip, an emissary of the FBI. Skip, a street person who noted, "I fit in that neighborhood" (*TD*, May 26, 1985), was amazed at how receptive the brothers were to his proffered friendship. On his first visit, James approached him and initiated a conversation. Skip later went out and bought beer. He came back and enjoyed friendly banter with the brothers about such subjects as sex and James Briley's new hairdo (*TD*, May 26, 1985).

On the Road to Freedom

CHAPTER 5

"The Blue Coated Mob on the Job"

The Search and Capture

> The T.V. screamed out the announcers' shout,
> "You better get indoors and lock your house!
> Shut out the lights, get your weapons out,
> Some *fool* motherfuckers are loose, running about!"
> It hit all the networks on the American scene,
> It hit South Africa, North Greenland and even Argentine,
> That the prison security model for the *whole* wide world
> Was *bust* wide open, split at the damn seams.
>
> Charles Satchell
> Virginia State Penitentiary, August 6, 1984

When Virginians discovered on June 1, 1984, that six condemned murderers and rapists had driven away from Mecklenburg's Death Row the night before, they reacted with a mixture of disbelief, indignation, anger, and fear, fanned by the constant sensationalization of the story in the front pages of the papers and as the lead story on newscasts during the ensuing weeks. The gruesome crimes for which the escapees were convicted were recounted daily, intensifying the widespread hysteria and creating a situation in many ways reminiscent of the situation in Virginia following Nat Turner's revolt.

Within hours of the discovery of the escape, one of the largest manhunts in the history of the state was underway, one involving before it would end the Virginia State Police, the FBI, the North Carolina Highway Patrol, the North Carolina National Guard, the North Carolina State Bureau of Investigations, the Royal Canadian Mounted Police, the Quebec Provincial Police, the Vermont State Troopers, and local police departments throughout the State

WANTED BY THE FBI

INTERSTATE FLIGHT — MURDER

LINWOOD EARL BRILEY

FBI No. 287 413 K4

Photograph taken 1980   Photograph taken 1980   Date photograph taken unknown

Aliases: Earl Briley, L. Briley, Lin Briley, Linny Briley, Linwood Briley, Linwood E. Briley, "Wolf"

DESCRIPTION

Date of Birth: March 26, 1954 (Birth data not supported by birth records)
Place of Birth: Richmond, Virginia
Height: 5' 9''
Weight: 150 to 170 pounds
Build: medium
Occupations: chauffeur, pay load operator
Scars and Marks: tattoos on left arm and left ear
Social Security Numbers Used: 230-82-4010; 230-82-3010; 230-30-1030
NCIC: PODIPMDM1517PO14DI14
Fingerprint Classification: 17 O 25 W IMM 15
            L 28 W OOI

Hair: black (wears mustache)
Eyes: brown
Complexion: medium
Race: Negro
Nationality: American

CRIMINAL RECORD

BRILEY HAS BEEN CONVICTED OF MURDER, RAPE AND ROBBERY.

CAUTION

LINWOOD BRILEY IS BEING SOUGHT AS AN ESCAPEE FROM THE MECKLENBURG CORRECTIONAL CENTER, WHERE HE WAS SERVING A LIFE SENTENCE FOR MURDER. CONSIDER BRILEY ARMED, EXTREMELY DANGEROUS AND AN ESCAPE RISK.

A Federal warrant was issued on June 1, 1984, at Richmond, Virginia, charging Linwood Briley with unlawful interstate flight to avoid confinement for the crime of murder (Title 18, U.S. Code, Section 1073).

IF YOU HAVE ANY INFORMATION CONCERNING THIS PERSON, PLEASE NOTIFY ME OR CONTACT YOUR LOCAL FBI OFFICE. TELEPHONE NUMBERS AND ADDRESSES OF ALL FBI OFFICES LISTED ON BACK.

William H. Webster

DIRECTOR
FEDERAL BUREAU OF INVESTIGATION
UNITED STATES DEPARTMENT OF JUSTICE
WASHINGTON, D.C. 20535
TELEPHONE: 202 324-3000

Entered NCIC
Wanted Flyer 520
June 14, 1984

WANTED BY THE FBI

INTERSTATE FLIGHT — MURDER

JAMES DYRAL BRILEY

FBI No. 773 047 CA8

Photograph taken 1980

Date photograph taken unknown

Date photograph taken unknown

Alias: James D. Briley

DESCRIPTION

Date of Birth: June 6, 1956 (Birth data not supported by birth records)
Place of Birth: Richmond, Virginia
Height: 6' 3''
Weight: 180 pounds
Build: slender
Occupation: laborer
Scars and Marks: scar over right eye; scar on left forearm; scar on stomach; Tattoo on left forearm
Social Security Number Used: 230-80-1873
NCIC: P063101313175513161 3
Fingerprint Classification: 13 O 1 R OII 13   Ref: 2
              L 17 R I00   17

Hair: black
Eyes: brown
Complexion: medium
Race: Negro
Nationality: American

CRIMINAL RECORD

BRILEY HAS BEEN CONVICTED OF MURDER, RAPE AND ROBBERY.

CAUTION

JAMES BRILEY IS BEING SOUGHT AS AN ESCAPEE FROM THE MECKLENBURG CORRECTIONAL CENTER, WHERE HE WAS SERVING A LIFE SENTENCE FOR MURDER. CONSIDER BRILEY ARMED, EXTREMELY DANGEROUS AND AN ESCAPE RISK.

A Federal warrant was issued on June 1, 1984, at Richmond, Virginia, charging James Briley with unlawful interstate flight to avoid confinement for the crime of murder (Title 18, U.S. Code, Section 1073).

IF YOU HAVE ANY INFORMATION CONCERNING THIS PERSON, PLEASE NOTIFY ME OR CONTACT YOUR LOCAL FBI OFFICE. TELEPHONE NUMBERS AND ADDRESSES OF ALL FBI OFFICES LISTED ON BACK.

William H. Webster

DIRECTOR
FEDERAL BUREAU OF INVESTIGATION
UNITED STATES DEPARTMENT OF JUSTICE
WASHINGTON, D.C. 20535
TELEPHONE: 202 324-3000

Entered NCIC
Wanted Flyer 519
June 14, 1984

of Virginia and in Warrenton and Henderson, North Carolina, Philadelphia, Pennsylvania, and in a host of other cities up and down the East Coast. The day following the escape Virginia's Governor Charles Robb issued an executive order placing the state's Army and Air National Guard units on alert, and, according to the *Times Dispatch*, the political leader of Quebec later suggested that the Canadian Army be called out (June 20, 1984, p. A-3). One FBI agent told me that with the cluster of airplanes and helicopters from the National Guard, the various Virginia authorities, the media, and several other agencies, "We almost needed air traffic controllers in Warrenton [population 1,063]" (June 21, 1985).

But the personal terror that obsessed individual Virginians and North Carolinians and later Canadians was in no way allayed by the law officials scanning the area in their infrared-equipped helicopters and small airplanes, and the hundreds of other rifle-toting law enforcement officials combing woods with their tracking dogs, scouring lakes in pontoon boats, and manning road blocks. Throughout areas where rumors of sightings of the escapees, but mainly the Brileys, were reported, citizens took desperate measures to protect themselves. It was noted that in the area where the Brileys lived in Richmond, children were afraid to play outside and adults no longer sat out on their porches. Residents in areas where hunts were concentrated sometimes moved out of their homes. Others barricaded themselves inside their houses and never went out. One Mecklenburg employee told me, "All community activities were cancelled—Girl Scouts didn't meet; pool parties were cancelled; a picnic we'd planned for the Girl Scouts had to be cancelled. All schools were on alert. The children became very nervous and jumpy and talked about it a lot. There were always rumors among them: 'Did you hear *the Briley brothers* were sighted!!! [delivered with a breathless, excited voice.]'" That same employee also told me of a scene she had witnessed in a local beauty salon: "About three weeks after the escape, I was in the hair dresser's when a little old white lady came in, just shaking all over, she was so nervous. She said this was her *first* trip out of the house. Every morning when her husband went out, she would lock the door and sit behind the door with a shotgun in her hand. But she said her hair had grown down over her eyes [indicating bangs covering her eyes] and so she had to risk coming to the hair dressers, but she was still shaking" (Mecklenburg, February 28, 1985). One guard at Mecklenburg told me, "My mother was in a panic; she took up a baseball bat and wrapped it in a towel, and got a butcher knife. She wouldn't go anywhere during that time without that bat and butcher knife" (Mecklenburg, February 28, 1985).

In some of the communities in Virginia and North Carolina where sightings occurred, people who had never locked their doors began not only locking—*and* barring—them, but sitting behind them with rifles and shotguns. Pictures appeared in the newspapers of little old ladies sitting on their porches with shotguns in their laps, of men standing outside their homes holding their rifles. Some citizens noted that they took pistols with them wherever they went. All around the state, but especially in the Mecklenburg County area and the Richmond area, an armed citizenry was anxiously preparing for a chance encounter with the escapees. One Mecklenburg employee said that because so many officers were in the field searching, other people sometimes had to assume some posts other than their regular assignments. Consequently, "One night I had to go out with a food service [employee] to take coffee, juice, and doughnuts to the guys out [searching] in an old state van. He's jumpy and he was wearing a pistol. I was scared to death. I wasn't scared of the Brileys; I was scared of him" (Mecklenburg, February 28, 1985). Another Black female official at Mecklenburg noted that because most of the men in Boydton were involved in the search, the women felt the need to provide protection for themselves and their families: "Whenever I went out of the house to take the trash or anything, I held a pistol in my hand like this [up in the air ready to aim] and I kept an ax by my bed" (Mecklenburg, February 28, 1985). Boydton residents, like one Warren County, North Carolina man, obviously operated by the credo, "I shoot first and ask questions later" (*TD*, June 4, 1984, p. A-5).

The paranoia was so great that a spokesman for the Virginia

"The Blue Coated Mob on the Job"

Department of Corrections warned that if he were a Black man living in the area around Warrenton, "I wouldn't walk in the woods and I wouldn't wear a blue shirt" (*NL*, June 6, 1984, p. 9). Another official at the penitentiary, commenting on the dangers posed because of the fear of a community armed to the hilt, noted that searchers were required to go up and knock on doors and that many of the searchers were tall, thin, Black men, wearing guard's uniforms, who were obviously afraid they would be killed. Mecklenburg personnel told me about a wealthy white man in the community who went home for lunch immediately after hearing about the escape. When he got into his house, a state van pulled up to his yard, and two Black guys in uniform started toward the front door. He ran to get a shotgun. They were there to inquire if he had seen the escapees. Wherever the escapees were suspected of being, young Black men were regarded with suspicion. One FBI agent told me that he had heard that some people in Warrenton, North Carolina, were wearing T-shirts with the logo, "I'm NOT one of the Briley Brothers." Indeed, given the widespread terror in the area and the ironical fact that the searchers so often resembled the fugitives, it is surprising that only one tragic accident occurred—and that had nothing to do with confusing searchers with fugitives. Alarmed when a man suspected of being one of the fugitives broke into a neighbor's house in Halifax County, North Carolina, and impressed by the gravity of the situation as he observed the helicopters flying overhead and the roadblock at the end of his street, one Halifax resident took out his gun, loaded it, and put it on the nightstand. Two days later his nine-year-old son was playing with a little three-year-old girl visiting next door. She asked if the gun were real, and the boy, planning to show her it was real, first removed the gun's clip, assuming that would make it safe; he then aimed the gun at her and fatally shot her between the eyes.

Not a few people were enjoying the excitement. Some men interviewed seemed to relish the possibility of an encounter and to boast about what they would do if the fugitives showed up at their homes. One Warren County resident, holding his gun at ready, asserted that if he saw an escapee, "I'd make it so hot for

Long Gone

him he wouldn't want to stay" (*TD*, June 4, 1984, p. A-5). Even a few women seemed to enjoy the media attention and the unwonted excitement that engulfed their small towns. The manager of the convenience store where the first escapees were captured in North Carolina reportedly exclaimed, "I love it. I could handle an earthquake. I love to be in the middle of things" (*NL*, June 2, 1984, p. 5). Other individuals apparently maliciously provoked media attention by reporting sightings or encounters with one of the escapees. One FBI agent told me of how investigators were frequently frustrated by reports from some people who fabricated sightings because they enjoyed the excitement created when hundreds of armed officers, helicopters, and dogs converged on an area in response and because they relished the opportunity this afforded them to be the center of attention.

The search was at first centered in the Warren County, North Carolina, area, where the abandoned van in which the men had driven from the Mecklenburg Correctional Center was found around midnight on May 31 and where a pickup truck was reported stolen during the night. Warrenton's agricultural fairgrounds on U.S. Route 158 were transformed into a command center for the searching agencies, and roadblocks were set up.

> Their first day of freedom had just begun.
> But it didn't last long for Derrick and Earl,
> The dumbest murderers in the world.
> Instead of making an attempt to flee,
> They stuck around to do their laundry.
> They were quite surprised as they sipped on their wine
> To hear a State Trooper say "Its back to Mecklenburg time."
>
> Anonymous photocopied toast
> circulating in FBI office

As soon as it was ascertained that the fugitives had crossed a state line, the FBI entered the case. They immediately began monitoring all telephone calls coming in and going out of Warrenton and quickly uncovered suspicious calls being made on the afternoon of June 1 from a public phone at Willoughby's Convenience Store and Laundromat, one block from the Warren County sheriff's department and jail. A group of officers went to the store

"The Blue Coated Mob on the Job"

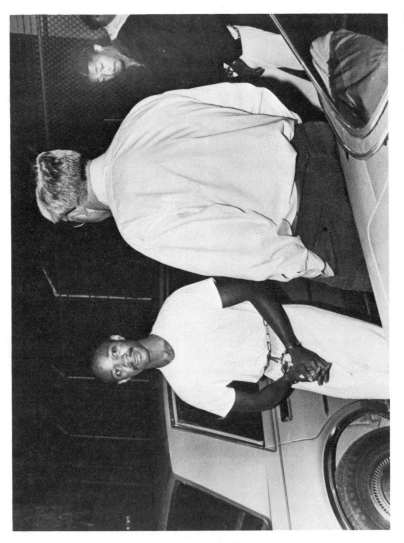

Derick Lynn Peterson (left) and Earl Clanton, Jr. (right) recaptured in Warrenton, North Carolina. Grateful acknowledgment is made to Richmond Newspapers, Inc., for permission to use this photograph.

but did not check the laundromat next door, where escapees Derick Lynn Peterson and Earl Clanton, Jr., were reportedly drinking and eating the wine and cheese and bread; one report indicated that they were eating pig's feet (*TD*, June 9, 1984, p. A-5) that they had purchased from the store next door. Peterson denies the accuracy of this report given in all newspaper accounts and confirmed by one of the arresting agents. He maintains, "No, I won't eating no cheese and no damn wine. . . . We had all that they said we had, but we wasn't eating.. . . I wasn't even hungry. Shit, I couldn't eat. You know how it is; you hungry when you ain't got nothing to eat. When I was in the woods, I was about to STARVE, right" (conversation, June 28, 1985). A few minutes later, at about 5:50 P.M., a special squad from the North Carolina Corrections Department and a Virginia State Trooper stormed the laundromat, ordered a cleaning woman there to stand back, and quickly apprehended the men. The unarmed fugitives were arrested without struggle; indeed one North Carolina official suggested that they were relieved to have been captured (*NL*, June 2, 1984, p. 1). The cleaning woman reported, however, that when they were apprehended the two escapees started arguing and one reproached the other, "You wanted me to come back in here like a——fool" (*TD*, June 20, 1984, p. A-3). Questioned by reporters, Peterson told of planning the escape for a year; asked why he was caught, he responded, "Damned if I know" (*TD*, June 20, 1984, p. A-3). He was later to tell me that he thinks his biggest mistake was staying with someone. Despite all of the planning, Clanton and Peterson had enjoyed only eighteen hours of freedom and had traveled only forty miles from the Mecklenburg Correctional Center.

On June 2, 1984, Governor Robb posted a $40,000 reward for information leading to the capture of the other four escapees.

Countless sightings of the inmates, especially the Brileys, continued to be reported throughout the state of Virginia as well as North Carolina. Upon news of such sightings, searching officials took to the air and the highways and byways with their tracking equipment, their weapons, and their dogs. Meanwhile the containment ring continued around Warren County, North Carolina.

"The Blue Coated Mob on the Job"

After the capture of the first two fugitives, however, the searchers in North Carolina and Virginia really had no promising leads.

> The bluecoated mob stayed on the job.
>
> "Gay Young Lad," *S&J*, p. 245

The searchers continued to check out every lead intensively, however, searching on the water, in the air, and on the ground. When there was a reported sighting of Linwood Briley at Hyco Reservoir in North Carolina (the Hyco Lake area is forty miles northwest of Oxford), helicopters and ground units went out in numbers. A shoulder to shoulder search of the area was conducted by 150 men dispatched to the area. All roads leading to the lake were blocked. This scenario was repeated ad infinitum. Frantic calls from frightened individuals throughout the two states continued to come in in large numbers, and police investigated all that they could. Police responded when a housewife in Charlotte County, Virginia, found two sets of underwear missing from her clothesline and checked out numerous other such calls from citizens who suspected the fugitives were in the vicinity, as well as some who claimed to have seen them or even been confronted by them, but police were not able to confirm any of the reported sightings. Indeed in many areas they were becoming frustrated by the unfounded reports of sightings that caused them to waste time. A Warrenton man reported a stolen shotgun one morning, only to report that afternoon that his mother had taken it. One frantic mother reported that one of the Brileys had demanded sex from her daughter only to have the daughter explain that her mother had misunderstood (*TD*, June 7, 1984, p. D-8). The Task Force and several Richmond police detectives were called from their beds at 2 A.M. one morning as a result of a tip that the Brileys were in a Richmond house; they rushed to surround the house where the Brileys were reportedly holed up, and maintained their surveillance until daybreak when they stormed the house and found it to be empty (interview, Sgt. Norman Harding, Richmond Police Department, June 5, 1985). These and other similar unfounded calls resulted in police making unwarranted arrests and needlessly surrounding homes and buildings,

Long Gone

A handcuffed Willie Leroy Jones being returned to Virginia. Grateful acknowledgment is made to Richmond Newspapers, Inc., for permission to use this photograph.

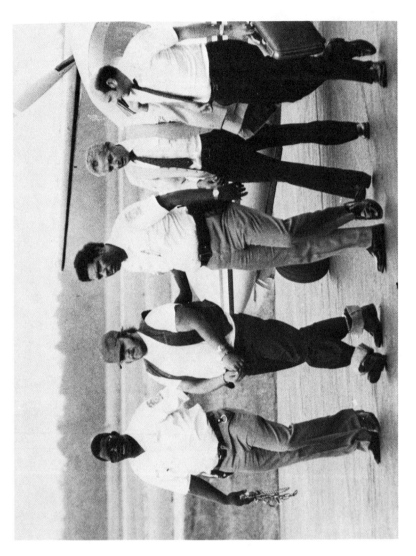

Lem Tuggle, in handcuffs, being returned to Virginia. Grateful acknowledgment is made to Richmond Newspapers, Inc., for permission to use this photograph.

setting up roadblocks, bringing in helicopters, and disbursing
large contingents of officials and bloodhounds.

By June 8, even the reports of sightings were dwindling.

> . . . Lem and Willie said Goodbye
> To the Briley boys, and to Vermont they did fly.
> Where the air is cool and the syrup sweet,
> They camped out in a tent as their retreat.
> But as time wore on and they didn't have a dime,
> Lem was forced to commit a crime.
> He stole some cash and made his geataway,
> But his freedom wouldn't last another day.
>
> Anonymous photocopied toast
> circulating in FBI office

In the meantime, Lem Tuggle had gotten to Vermont, where he bought some clothes in an army/navy store. He also had a coat a woman had given him. By June 8 he was within ten miles of the Canadian border, but he was broke, having spent needed money for food and clothes for Jones, who Tuggle told me had no funds.[1] Desperate for money to finance his trip to Canada, he went to the Red Mill Gift Shop in Woodford, Vermont, shortly after 12 noon on Friday, June 8. He held a knife to the throat of the shop's operator and robbed her of $100 (the knife used here was not from Mecklenburg—those knives had been discarded long ago: "I had gotten another one" [conversation, Tuggle, June 28, 1985]). When he drove off she noted the number of the pickup truck that he was driving, and called the police.[2] After a brief chase, Tuggle was stopped at a road block. He was captured by the only law enforcement officer in Stamford, the part-time constable whose previous police work involved "kid stuff" like stolen bicycles (TD, June 9, 1984, p. 1); his was such a quiet town that he had not even had an armed robbery since he had held his post. When he stopped Tuggle and held a gun on him, Tuggle, who was armed with a knife, offered no resistance. The arresting officer was shocked to discover that he had apprehended one of the subjects of the extensive manhunt that seemed so far removed from him: "I'll probably faint when it hits me who he really is,"

"The Blue Coated Mob on the Job"

he observed shortly after the capture (*TD*, June 9, 1985, p. 1). Taken into custody shortly after 1 P.M. on Friday, June 8, Tuggle had been free ten days. The sheriff of Smith County, Virginia, Tuggle's home and the site of the murders for which he was convicted, warned Vermont authorities, "Do y'all have him in a secure place? You'd better have. He's got a real knack for making weapons out of anything. I wouldn't trust him as far as I can throw New York" (*NL*, June 13, 1984, p. 4).

> Not far from there a call went out in earnest
> From Willie Leroy to Mommie Dearest
> "Willie, please come home," she said with a cry,
> "Turn yourself in before you die."
>
> Anonymous photocopied toast
> circulating in FBI office

Later that same afternoon, Willie Leroy Jones, who had been with Tuggle until that morning and whom Tuggle said probably couldn't make it on his own (July 8, 1985), broke into a house in the border town of Jay, Vermont, and called his mother in Richmond. She talked him into surrendering. He then called the Vermont State Police, and turned himself in to them about 6:45 P.M. on June 8. He had eighty- eight cents when he was captured. Jones too had had ten days of freedom.

> All that was left was the Briley brothers,
> but everybody knew they were badder than the others.
> The question was Where could they be?
> Carolina, Quebec or old Virginny?
>
> Anonymous photocopied toast
> circulating in FBI office

Reports leaked following the arrests of Tuggle and Jones that they had dropped the Brileys off in Richmond on their trek north. Although authorities denied these reports, they sparked any number of renewed reportings of sightings of the Brileys in Richmond, reports which kept Richmond police busy for several days. The discovery of two of the convicts so close to Canada also sparked rumors that the Brileys has escaped to Canada, and Canada called out the Quebec Provincial Force and Vermont called out its state troopers, who conducted extensive and intensive sweeps of the border area. Rumors circulated that the Brileys had gone toward Montreal, inciting intense fear among the citizens of that city. The sight of two Black men seemed enough to drive people in the area into a frenzy. One delivery man making a delivery of chicken dropped his delivery and ran without his money when he noted that the recipients were two Negroes. He called the police and reported that he had seen the Brileys. This scenario was repeated over and over in the border area of Canada.

On June 11, the command post in Warrenton was closed down and a new command post was established in Clarksville, Virginia.

> People said they saw them everywhere down South,
> In woods, in the hills.
> Hell the brothers was up in Philly drinking and
>   eating ribs.
>
> Harry Seigler
Mecklenburg, March 1985

Daily reports of citings of the Brileys continued. During their escape they were variously sighted in Montreal, Philipsburg, and Bedford, Canada; in Boston; in New York; in Hanover, Bracey, Portsmouth, and Richmond, Virginia; in Henderson, Granville, Warren County, and Oxford, North Carolina; and elsewhere. Throughout their flight it indeed seemed that "Everybody is Linwood Briley."

The front page coverage of the story continued in the Richmond papers, focusing on the search for the Brileys in the border area after the capture of Tuggle and Jones in Vermont. The fact that the prime focus of the search for the brothers was now centered in Philadelphia was unannounced in the media and unknown to the public until the headlines of June 21 announced their capture in Philadelphia on the previous night.

Following the escape from Mecklenburg, Richmond police and the FBI began checking their files for information on friends and family of the Brileys, whom they checked and in some instances tailed. They also placed lookouts at critical places where the Brileys might be expected to go to seek refuge or to seek vengeance.

"The Blue Coated Mob on the Job"

Guards were assigned to protect some prosecutors and witnesses in the Briley cases as well as their families, especially the Meekins family, whose son had been the major witness against them.

Investigators checked people who had called or visited the Brileys while they were in prison. FBI Agent Jim Trotter combed the telephone records from Mecklenburg and discovered that there were several calls to the telephone of their uncle in Philadelphia. It was also discovered that calls had been made from that Philadelphia number to the Briley home in Richmond following the escape. The Richmond FBI office attempted to send the uncle's telephone number to their Philadelphia office for investigation, but a series of blunders occurred that were ironically to prove fortunate. The Richmond office mistakenly transposed two numbers. The Philadelphia agents went to the home of the subscribers to the number they had received, and reported that they knew nothing about the Briley brothers or any calls to or from them. So the Richmond office sent them another number, but again two numbers were transposed. The Philadelphia agents went to the home of the subscriber to the second number, but they knew nothing about the calls either. They reported that to the Richmond office, and the Richmond office again transmitted the number of the uncle. By this time other information had resulted in the surveillance of the uncle's home and the garage where they were later captured, and so the agents did not go to his home. Ironically, had they been given the correct number in the first place and gone to his home, the Briley brothers might have been alerted and would probably have gotten away (interview, June 19, 1985).

Agent Michael Carbonell of the Philadelphia FBI had been assigned the Briley case for his area the day after the escape (such cases are routinely assigned to the FBI offices in many cities): "At that time I had no idea they would end up in Philadelphia" (interview, June 25, 1985). Soon, however, all leads began to point to the Philadelphia area, and Agent Carbonell became convinced that the Brileys were there, though he had not seen them. Richmond police had also received telephone tips that the Briley brothers were in Philadelphia. Additionally, information reportedly provided by Lem Tuggle indicated that the Briley brothers had been dropped off at a park near the uncle's home. The uncle's home on North Seventh Street was placed under surveillance, and FBI agents observed him leaving with an individual who they thought was Linwood (*TD*, May 26, 1985, p. A-2). It was the tailing of the uncle that ultimately led them to the garage where the brothers were staying. Finally, investigators had received information that an acquaintance of the brothers in New York had received a telephone call from them, and they were able to trace the call to the same garage. FBI agents in a van began to maintain constant surveillance of the garage, which was in the 2400 block of North Second Street, but they did not want to move precipitately and blow the case—"We go slow and easy" (Carbonell).

They called in a bounty hunter and assigned him the task of befriending the suspects, determining if they were indeed the Brileys, and, if so, setting them up for the arrest. The plant, known as Skip, completed his assignment flawlessly. The episode was reminiscent of "Honky Tonk Bud," where a bounty hunter appears in much the same manner as Skip, who just walked up to the garage. In the toast, "Hip Bud. . . suddenly dug / A stranger moving his way." Like Bud in that toast, James Briley made an immediate friendly move toward the stranger: "Now hip [Bud] started to grin, and he said, "Like, uh, er, dig this, my man, / My name is Stud from 'cross the way, / I may kin do some good for you." That toast ends predictably when a cat pulls out a badge and says, "Freeze, I'm the F.B.I.!" (*S&J*, pp. 237–38).

After initiating a conversation with the brothers at the garage on the evening of the arrest, Skip left a couple of times, and each time he left, he reported to Carbonell.[3] Positive identification was made difficult by the poor quality of the pictures that had been provided to the FBI, but Skip finally reported that he was "almost positive" that one of the men at the garage was Linwood Briley. Soon afterward surveillants observed the uncle drive up to the garage. They were confident now that the men at the garage were the Brileys, and they decided to make their move.

"The Blue Coated Mob on the Job"

Who would think
That the old fried chick
so mutta futta mean
so dame lean
that the smell
could bring out the tails
of those brileys
in the name of God
don't ever give me a chick
compared to the FBI
that chick was so. . .
mighty got dame slick.

Larry Batten, Mecklenburg Correctional Center
March 24, 1985

They was sittin' in there shuffling them broads [cards],
   sippin' that gin. . .
That's when them goddamn rollers start tippin' back in.

"Stag," *S&J*, p. 229

   The brothers were milling around in and out of the garage with several other people standing on the sidewalk in front, chatting, drinking beer, and barbecuing chicken; among those present were their uncle, Skip, and the owner of the garage. When he saw that both brothers were outside the garage, an FBI lookout gave the signal, and an FBI special weapons team of more than twenty men sped to the scene in a van and two cars. As the speeding vehicles screeched to a halt, agents bounded out, shotguns drawn, screaming, "FBI! Freeze!" and swooped down upon James and Linwood Briley. The first agent out of the van was Agent Carbonell. He pointed his gun at James Briley and ordered him to lie down. He handcuffed him and raised his shirt to look for the old bullet wound he knew he had. Not until he saw the scar was he sure of the identity of his captive. Momentarily, Linwood Briley was also seized. Carbonell was shocked that, given the precipitance with which so large a contingent of agents had swooped down upon them, the brothers showed none of the alarm that most people would have exhibited: "Most people would have been frightened . . . but those guys struck me as

Long Gone

being very cold and ruthless people—they weren't scared at all—
even considering the way we came in. If they had had weapons, we would probably have had a shootout." As it was they did not resist arrest at all, but they were cool and composed, though they feigned surprise. James asked, "Hey, what's going on. Hey, brother, what's going on?" They initially denied that they were the Brileys. Later, when it was clear that their identity was established, Linwood told Carbonell that the only murder he had committed was the accidental murder of his neighbor and that "he was framed because he was Black." The Brileys had enjoyed exactly nineteen days of freedom.

When Corrections Director Landon was told of the capture, he reportedly exclaimed, "My God, it's the end of a nightmare. Somebody turned on the lights in the world" (*NL*, June 20, 1984, p. 1). But the nightmare was not over for Landon, the State Corrections System, or the Robb administration.

The Brileys were driven from Philadelphia to Richmond in two marshalls' service cars which were escorted by state police from all the jurisdictions along the way; they were taken to the Virginia State Penitentiary where they were reunited with their fellow escapees. Tuggle told me there were no recriminations among the group: "Nobody blamed anybody else" for being caught. When I asked if any expressed regrets about anything regarding the escape, he laughed and responded, "No, the only thing we were sorry about was that we got caught" (July 8, 1985). Peterson likewise noted that nobody held anyone else accountable for what had gone wrong. On the contrary, everybody recognized what he had done wrong and where they had not planned enough what they would do when they got out. He said the Brileys considered it their fault that they had remained in one place too long. Even though they all heard that Tuggle had done some talking when he was captured that might have provided information that assisted the authorities in locating the Brileys, Peterson maintained, "They didn't blame it on nobody but themselves." He did note, however, that they had all previously agreed not to talk to anybody, especially not to the press, and that they were "surprised" that Tuggle gave an interview. Follow-

"The Blue Coated Mob on the Job"

ing newspaper accounts of his role in providing information about the escape, Tuggle was kept separated from his cohorts in another prison. When the one-year anniversary reports of the escape reported details of Tuggle's role in providing information about the escape, Tuggle, then in Mecklenburg, was again moved back to the Virginia State Penitentiary. He has since been returned to Mecklenburg.

Long Gone

CHAPTER 6

"I Raised Hell While I Was There"

The Effects of the Escape on the Prison System

In his eternal conflicts with his white opponent, the Black folk character rarely, even in the yarns of the most imaginative storytellers and singers, achieves much more than a temporary victory. But to cause even momentary discomfort, embarrassment, or defeat for his all-powerful enemy and to achieve even fleeting power, freedom, or control is frequently enough to bring great pleasure to Black bards and their audiences, as is suggested in the old tale of the Black man in heaven. (It is important to remember that in these tales heaven is often a reproduction of racist America, and God is just another Big White Boss such as they have suffered under in America.)

> This Black man died and he went to heaven. And he was so glad to get to heaven. Saint Peter was giving out the wings, and he was so happy 'cause he had made it, he decided he would get his wings himself; so he picked up two wings—didn't care which two—whether they were right or wrong. But it was two left wings. And he put 'em on. He was flying all one-sided, *all* 'round the walls, knocking down things. Saint Peter say, "HEY!" Say, "Come here." He say, "*Who* gave you those wings?"
>
> He say, "I put 'em on myself."
>
> He say, "Now look, you niggers done tore up earth. You not coming up here and tear up heaven. Just gimme those wings!"
>
> He say, "Well, I had a flying good time while I had 'em on though!"
>
> *S&J*, pp. 13–14

[Variant ending] "Well, they put me out," he says, "but, HEY! HEY! I raised hell while I was there."

S&J, p. 13

[While they were out, the Brileys] enjoyed everything that was happening.... They did it up right, they did a lot of things—maybe that they shouldn't have done. They enjoyed themselves. I'm glad they did.

Fellow escapee Derick Peterson,
June 28, 1985

The Brileys and their cohorts may have achieved freedom and control of their lives only temporarily, but through their flight they caused more embarrassment and problems and upheavals and inspections and studies in the State Correctional System all the way up to the office of the governor than any other event during the administration of Charles (Chuck) Robb—and the repercussions continue. (It is interesting to recall that similarly the revolt of Nat Turner was the most critical event of the administration of then-Governor John Floyd.[1])

From the moment the escape was discovered and Virginians woke up appalled to find that SIX convicted felons had DRIVEN out of a maximum security prison, shocked and angry citizens began casting blame everywhere from the prison guards to the governor. And despite the fact that many of those in all of these ranks, including numerous prison guards and even the secretary of Transportation and Public Safety (which oversees the Department of Corrections), were Black, it is important to note that historically the folk perceive those who work within the system in such positions as conspirators with the enemy, often regarding them with more hostility and attacking them with more vehemence than they do their white counterparts. Such has been the attitude toward Black overseers in slavery, and later toward Black policemen and prison guards.

Initially higher officials seemed to encourage the tendency to place the blame on the guards, who were accused of being poorly trained, of being unfamiliar with the prescribed procedures such as the guidelines for dealing with a bomb threat, who failed to carry out the most basic, routine requirements such as periodi-

Long Gone

cally counting prisoners, who disregarded critical rules regarding the opening of control room doors,[2] and who meekly surrendered to the rebels without resistance. Later, inmates would taunt the guards about their fear and ineptness during the escape:

> [Every time one inmate sees the lieutenant who told the tower guard to open the gates, he screams], "Open those goddamn gates, in the name of God, let these niggers go." Everyone laughs because the inmate usually dramatizes it with falling on the floor holding his neck with his eyes wide open like he's in fear and shaking.
>
> Take the guards that were top ranked officers before the escape, the ones that were demoted, inmates joke them by saying, "Will you please pass this book on the other side?" Or "Can I borrow your pants and shirt if you don't mind?" Or "There's some guy in the bathroom who needs to see you."
>
> I heard one guy tell some guards, "That's why the guys escaped, you dumb mother fuckers don't know your ass from a hole in the ground. I got to be one dumb mother fucker myself not to be long gone by now, because you mother fuckers ain't got enough sense to keep a baby in a crib."
>
> Letter from a Mecklenburg inmate,
March 14, 1985

One Death Row inmate wrote to the *News Leader* that the "guards are totaly [sic] untrained [and]. . . not physically fit at all" (June 18, 1984, p. 3). The alleged incompetence of guards during the escape and in later incidents was frequently derided by higher-ups as well. House Speaker A. Philpott asserted, "The prisoner is so much more intelligent than the guards they are able to manipulate the guards rather than the other way around" (*TD*, September 15, 1984, p. B-1). In a debate in the legislature on Robb's proposal to raise the salaries of Virginia's prison guards, one delegate inquired whether the higher paid guards would be "able to count to six when they put [prisoners] out and count to six when they bring them back" (*NL*, January 11, 1985, p. 1; the reference is to the failure to note that one prisoner was missing when the inmates were brought in from recreation immediately prior to the escape). Initially also many people inside and outside

"I Raised Hell While I Was There"

the correctional system suspected that some guards must have given aid to the escapees.

Guards, defensive, sensitive, and embarrassed, angrily rejected accusations that *they* were responsible for the escape and blamed the administrators of the correctional system for trying to shift the blame from themselves. They retorted that there were flaws in the design of the prison, that there were inadequate guards, and that the turnover was too great, largely because of the poor pay received, and that they were restricted in their ability to exercise any authority as a result of a 1983 settlement of a class-action suit, *Brown* vs. *Procunier*, in which the American Civil Liberties Union had forced some changes and won some rights for and eased some restrictions upon the prisoners.[3] They were not without their supporters for all of these charges, and even some administrators joined them in alleging that the settlement had created a situation wherein the ACLU and the inmates were running the prison. When I asked then-Corrections Director Robert M. Landon if the *Brown* vs. *Procunier* settlement had had an effect on the operations at Mecklenburg, he responded, "Certainly psychologically" (interview, July 12, 1984). Virginia newspapers frequently supported the contention that prison discipline was disrupted by *Brown* vs. *Procunier* and other ACLU suits. The editorial in the *News Leader* on August 7, 1984, titled "Who's in Charge?" insisted that events at Mecklenburg, beginning with the escape, give prisoners an "impression they have the upper hand." Thus, the writer continued, "They become dissatisfied with prison life, so they call the ACLU. They raise a ruckus, and prison guards and administrators get disciplined" (p. 10). Like Landon, most objective observers and outside reviewers insist that while it is clear that the agreement has had an impact on staff morale because they perceive it as allowing the inmates to govern the prison, there is no evidence that the terms of the settlement have contributed to the problems at Mecklenburg. In a ruling relative to problems at Mecklenburg, U.S. District Judge Robert R. Merhige, Jr., asserted that the ACLU class action suit had "not the slightest thing to do" with the escape and asserted that those charges "border on the ridiculous" (*TD*, October 3,

The "Report of the Mecklenburg Correctional Center
Study Committee" (November 7, 1984) found that the ACLU settlement agreement has "taken on an importance in DOC [Department of Corrections] and among employees at MCC [Mecklenburg Correctional Center] which is greatly misplaced and out of proportion to what the agreement in fact provides" (pp. 154–55).

The administration staffs at Mecklenburg and the Corrections Department also received their share of the blame for the escape. Regarding the escapes from Virginia penitentiaries, the *News Leader* sarcastically inquired, "Is Virginia running a prison system, or a sieve?" (editorial, July 11, 1984, p. 10).

The Great Escape was a thorn in the side of Governor Chuck Robb from the moment he was awakened before 2 A.M. on June 1, 1984, and informed of the debacle until he reported on his four-year term in office in December 1985 and noted that the event "virtually paralyzed the department" (*TD*, December 26, 1985, p. 1). Beginning with his first response, whatever reaction he made to the events stemming from that event provoked extensive debate and criticism. On the first day following the escape, he noted that state government was practically immobilized as he "cancelled the schedule and set up a command post" in his office (quoted in the *TD*, June 12, 1984, p. A-5). Later he had to assure that other business of the state was not being put on hold by the focus on the problem at Mecklenburg. The *Washington Post* reported that almost a year after the escape Robb flinches every time the telephone rings in the middle of the night: "The first thought is that it has something to do with the corrections system, but I'm not paranoid" (May 28, 1985, p. 1). Throughout, Republicans were unrelenting in their determination to make the prison problem a major issue in the fall 1985 statewide races. Almost every event in the ongoing crisis was seized upon by them, especially by one of the prospective Republican gubernatorial candidates, as ammunition for additional attacks on the Democratic administration. At their state convention in Hampton in June 1984, Republicans loudly deplored the escape and criticized the Robb administration and its inadequate response to the situation. Their criticism was not tempered as the Robb administration and the correctional system, responding to criticisms of laxness, enacted strict restrictions, including the wiretapping of telephone calls from Death Row and the limitation of access to lawyers. The senate minority leader than charged, "Mecklenburg-gate [implies] the pendulum has swung from grave laxity in security to an overzealousness" (*TD*, February 12, 1985, p. 3). Wherever he went Robb could not escape the barbs about the escape. At dinners and parties and social and political events he had to grin politely at gibes such as this by Phil Bagley, former mayor of Richmond:

> The governor has put in a new system that he says will save a lot of money on the prison food bills. Each day at sundown the guard has to go to each prisoner and say, "The cook wants to know, are you planning to be here for breakfast?"
>
> Quoted in the *TD*, February 24, 1985, p. C- 1

Republicans were not the only ones who held the Robb administration accountable. On June 11 the Mecklenburg County Board of Supervisors expressed outrage at the escape and voted unanimously to write to the governor and ask him to "get your house in order" (*TD*, June 12, 1984, p. 1).

Others blamed the lengthy process of appeals in capital cases for the escape. Typical was an editorial in the *News Leader* that insisted it is "beside the point" to ask who is to blame in the breakout: the problem is procrastination in trying and executing criminals." They went on to note, "The Brileys. . . were at Mecklenburg for murders they committed in the late Seventies. Why are they still around? Why have the taxpayers housed them and fed them and paid to have them guarded for five years?" A speedy execution within eighteen months "would be one way to reduce the possibility of a recurrence of what happened at Mecklenburg last week," they concluded (June 4, 1984, p. 10). In a later editorial in the same vein following the capture the writer "deplore[d] the larger failures of a society abiding a system of 'justice' that keeps creeps like the Brileys alive in fancy facilities for seemingly ever and a day" (*NL*, June 20, 1984, p. 14).

Long Gone

In an effort to determine the facts of the escape and to ascertain where the blame did indeed lie, to prevent future occurrences and to allay public outrage, numerous study groups and commissions were appointed. Within a few days a report was prepared by Mecklenburg Warden Gary L. Bass (June 5, 1984); and that was followed by a report prepared by the Department of State Police (July 3, 1984). Four reports were commissioned by the secretary of Transportation and Public Safety with resources provided by the United States Department of Justice's National Institute of Corrections. These reports were submitted to the secretary in June and July. Following a highly publicized and controversial shakedown at Mecklenburg on July 26, an internal Department of Corrections investigation was begun.

Possibly prompted by the continuing criticism of Republican leaders as well as the concerns of some Democrats, on August 14, 1984, a study commission was appointed to probe the escape and to consider such matters as the pay of prison employees and other problems. Even the appointment of the committee created controversy. Donald W. Huffman, chairman of the Republican party of Virginia, resigned before the committee could begin deliberations, noting that service on the committee placed him in a no-win situation since he would be accused of partisanship if the report of the committee were critical of the Democratic administration and that the Republicans would criticize him for supporting the Democrats if the committee's report supported the Robb administration's handling of the situation. Republicans greeted news of the committee with the complaint that the committee was the equivalent of the "corrections department investigating itself" (Marshall Coleman, quoted in the *NL*, August 15, 1984, p. 13; the committee was made up of five of the members of the Board of Corrections, appointed by the chairman of the board at the request of Governor Robb).

The reports of the warden and of the Department of State Police detailed the events at the penitentiary during the escape and the role of individual inmates and guards in that drama. Generally, most of the commissioned reports conducted by authorities from outside the state cited problems in the design of

"I Raised Hell While I Was There"

the facility, in the administration and management of the institution, in the morale of the personnel, in the interaction between inmates and staff, and in the failure of the guards to be familiar with certain rules and guidelines and to properly enforce others. Although they found the performance of the guards deplorable, they judged their training adequate and discovered no evidence of complicity between the guards and inmates in the escape. One report, stating that collusion was unlikely, implied that it was unnecessary since "routine practices of the staff were so reliably poor that it degraded the security effort to the point where the inmates were able to successfully work it to their advantage."[4] Numerous recommendations were made in all of the studies. Among them were recommendations for extensive revisions in security, including the installation of mirrors in halls and around perimeter guard towers, the installation of television cameras, the use of body alarms by guards, the blocking off of empty spaces behind stairwells, the interlocking of sally ports so that only one gate can open at a time, and the changing of the locks on restroom doors. They recommended also that contact at prescribed intervals between control posts and master control be required, that periodic checks be made of compliance with new standards, that the number of official counts be increased to a minimum of five per day, that supervisory visibility in Death Row and other high security sections be increased, and that smoke detection equipment and a sprinkler system be installed. They suggested improvement in management and supervisory training and increased job, recreational and educational opportunities for inmates. At least one of them pointed to the urgent need to improve sanitation at the prison. Several of these recommendations have already been implemented.

The Mecklenburg Correctional Center Study Committee found that many sources shared responsibility for the problems at Mecklenburg, including the Board of Corrections. They observed that some corrections had been accomplished since the escape, but that much remained to be done and made several recommendations for improving the operation of the facility at all levels.

The internal Department of Corrections investigation commissioned as a result of the July 26 shakedown found that some inmates were brutalized during the shakedown.

Clearly the admissions of responsibility, the resignations, and the firings that have continually occurred since the escape have been at least partially prompted by the critical findings of these studies of the escape and of the situation at Mecklenburg.[5] The day before the first report, on June 4, 1984, sixteen correctional personnel were placed on paid administrative leave, pending the investigation of the escape. Some staff at Mecklenburg resigned, reportedly because of the dangerous, lenient environment there. On June 12 the resignation of the chief nurse and two of her assistants was reported. They noted that they had written to Governor Robb more than a year before complaining about the risks to which they were daily subjected, but that they had not received any response (*TD*, June 12, p. A-5). By mid-August at least twelve prison employees had resigned for causes related to the takeover (*NL*, August 13, 1984, p. 1). On June 22 a Mecklenburg guard who resigned on the previous day was arrested and charged with selling marijuana to an inmate on Death Row. On that same day the warden, the assistant warden for operations, and the chief of security were relieved of their duties, not for personal failures, it was announced, but because of the fact that the staff had been demoralized by the escape and the institution required new leadership "to restore community confidence" (Landon, quoted in the *NL*, June 23, p. 5). The three were to be assigned to other posts in the Correctional System. Warden Gary Bass responded that he was not upset about the transfer, but that he was disturbed that he and the other two members of his staff had to hear about their transfer on the radio (*NL*, June 23, 1984, p. 5). On July 1 approximately seventy correctional officials deliberating on the escapes were warned by Corrections Director Landon that wardens would lose their jobs if they were not able to stem the tide of breakouts. On July 5, the same day that three of the commissioned studies were submitted to the secretary of Transportation and Public Safety, five guards involved in the escape were fired, two for having left control rooms during the escape and three for failing to count or search inmates returning

"I Raised Hell While I Was There"

from recreation. On that same day as well two members of the Mecklenburg administration who had been relieved earlier were placed on temporary disciplinary suspension. On August 9, one guard, who had already submitted his resignation (effective August 16) because of the dangerous situation at Mecklenburg, was trapped in Building No. 5 during a riot. He was hit and had his neck twisted and was sure that he would be killed: "I had already died. I was just waiting for it" (*TD*, August 9, 1984, p. 1). On August 10, two of the guards accused of brutality against inmates during a July 26 shakedown were fired and a third received temporary disciplinary suspension. Both of the guards, who insisted that they were being made scapegoats, were later ordered rehired.

Several of the guards fired or disciplined protested or filed appeals; some of them were quietly reinstated.

The heads that rolled as a result of this escape were not limited to Mecklenburg personnel. Ultimately, a series of officials issued statements acknowledging responsibility on the part of administration and management for the escape, admissions that were remarkably coincidental with either their own decisions to resign or the decisions of other upper-level administrators to resign, though in most instances those who offered resignations and their superiors denied that the resignations were under duress. On August 20, Secretary of Transportation and Public Safety Franklin E. White reported that the escape was the result of "massive failure of management and supervision." (White resigned almost a year later [effective July 5, 1985] to accept a position as commissioner of the Department of Transportation, Albany, New York.) On November 23 Governor Robb announced the resignation of Corrections Department Chief Robert M. Landon, effective December 1, and the appointment of Allyn R. Sielaff, his deputy secretary of Public Safety, to that post. Landon's November 16, 1984, letter of resignation was written nine days after the submission of the report of the Mecklenburg Correctional Center Study Committee, but it was not immediately made public. Robb insisted that Landon's resignation was "at his own initiative" (quoted in the *TD*, November 24, 1984, p. 1). In

one interview Landon explained that the "bottom line" cause of
his resignation was that "I just couldn't extricate myself from the
Mecklenburg death row escape" (quoted in the *TD*, November
24, 1984, p. 1). On November 28 he declared, "I was the skipper
of the S.S. Mecklenburg when it went under. I did my best, but I
guess the best wasn't good enough" (Channel 12 News, November 28, 1984). In May 1985 Warden Elwood L. Booker, the first
Black warden at the Virginia State Penitentiary, announced his
resignation, citing personal reasons. This resignation, following
highly publicized escapes, lockdowns, uprisings, and the executions of the Brileys at his institution, was naturally attributed to
those events by some observers, including Corrections Director
Sielaff (see *NL*, May 22, 1985, p. 17). In December 1985 Sielaff
announced his resignation. Both he and Robb denied allegations
that he was pushed into resigning.

Throughout all of this time, additional prison escapes, uprisings, and unrest occurred that contributed to the many resignations and firings and that seemed to have been sparked by the
Great Escape; even those activities that might have been considered normal and expected in the routine of prison life and that
ordinarily would have received little or no press coverage received
more exposure because of the Great Escape. Thus daily, the accounts of prison turmoil provoked more anguished and persistent
demands from the public that something be done about the "un-
controllable" situation in Virginia's prisons, and each new episode
was followed by some new proclamation from officials designed
to assure the public that such events would not recur.

On June 9, 1984, little more than a week after the escape, a
cache of weapons was discovered on Death Row at Mecklenburg.
On June 11 an inmate at the Staunton Correctional Center attempted to take a nurse hostage, noting that he hoped to get
publicity for his appeal. On June 15 a man who claimed to be a
cousin of the Brileys abducted a woman, her two children, and a
friend from a shopping mall in South Richmond. On June 16
three inmates escaped from Trenton State Prison, whose superintendent, coincidentally, was one of the three national corrections experts whom Governor Robb had called in to investigate

the Mecklenburg escape. On June 19 an inmate at Mecklenburg stabbed a guard. On June 20 it was announced that a knife had been found on Death Row during an investigation of the escape. On June 29 two maximum-security inmates ran away from their work detail outside the State Penitentiary, prompting Governor Robb to order that maximum-security inmates no longer be allowed to work on such details. On that same day it was reported that a search at Mecklenburg uncovered hand-made weapons and cut-window struts, suggesting preparations for another escape. On July 6 an inmate's neck was broken while he was playing basketball at Mecklenburg; there was some question about whether his death was caused by accident or intent and whether it was related to the escape. On July 10 a trusty convicted of rape and two other felonies ran away from a work detail near Baskerville, about ten miles from the Mecklenburg Correctional Center. On July 12 several inmates and guards were injured in an uprising at Mecklenburg; the inmates in Building No. 1, the same building which houses Death Row, armed themselves with metal taken from weight machines and barbells as well as wood from picnic tables and refused to leave the recreation yard. They were subdued by guards using mace. Then, after watching the fray, inmates in Building No. 2 decided to take their guards hostage. As they beat the resisting guards, reinforcements arrived and put down the rebels. At the time of this confrontation, I was interviewing Landon in his Richmond office, and he was several times interrupted to be informed of the situation. He suggested that the inmates may have been testing the new warden. On July 13 a series of shakedowns began in Building No. 3 at Mecklenburg, uncovering numerous weapons as well as marijuana. It was also discovered that attempts had been made to saw through supporting structures in the windows of some cells in the building. On July 26 a shakedown at Mecklenburg supported by fifty guards from Nottoway Correctional Center resulted in the discovery of several weapons and in charges of brutality by the Nottoway guards. As many as twenty-six prisoners were reported injured during the search. Later Landon was to confirm the accusations of deliberate and premeditated violence on the part

Long Gone

of a few of the guards brought in to assist in the shakedown; he said that some of the guards from Nottoway asked for the location of specific prisoners: "They went to their cells and they assaulted them, plain and simple, brutalized them" (*TD*, August 21, 1984, p. B-1). On September 3, juveniles attempting to escape from the Richmond city jail in a plot perceived as being motivated by the Great Escape jammed their doors so that they registered as secure on the control panel; then one of them lured a guard to his cell whereupon the other prisoners opened their cell doors and jumped him. They then went to the control box and opened all the cells in the cellblock. The escape was foiled, but the guard was killed. On August 4 a group of maximum-security inmates at Mecklenburg, reacting to the violence during the July 26 shakedown and to increased restrictions as a result of the escape, used their handcuffs to threaten choking a guard who made the mistake of turning his back on an inmate. They took additional hostages and held them overnight, demanding action to allieviate the "barbaric treatment here at this institution." Among their demands were an end to the harrassment of Death Row inmates and the return of typewriters to those inmates. Ironically the first demands in this uprising came from a Death Row inmate—and they were typed, though typewriters were removed from Death Row after the escape. During this uprising some of the same techniques of the Great Escape were employed, suggesting that the original intent of some involved was to escape: three prison control rooms were taken over by inmates, and inmates undressed officers and put on their uniforms (*NL*, August 7, 13, 1984, pp. 1, 5). Three correctional officials were seriously injured during this uprising. On September 7 a minor uprising at Buckingham Correctional Center resulted in injury to one guard. On September 9, inmates demanding a transfer from Brunswick Correctional Center held a guard hostage for several hours. On November 22 five inmates escaped from the new Nottoway Correctional Center. On January 7, 1985, a convicted murderer had himself boxed with envelopes from the print shop of the penitentiary and was driven out in a truck, a feat reminiscent of the legendary escape of slave Henry "Box" Brown, who

"I Raised Hell While I Was There"

escaped from Richmond in a similar manner. On April 13, prisoners at the Virginia State Penitentiary, attempting to take hostages to prevent the execution of James Briley, injured nine guards. They targeted four guards for attack, three of whom were on the team to carry out executions (*NL*, November 15, 1985, p. 19). The lockdown which followed that uprising, lasting from April 18 to May 17, was one of the longest lockdowns in the prison's history. On May 5, 1985, three inmates at the Powhatan Correctional Center attempted to escape by hiding in the recreational yard when fellow inmates returned from recreation. They had left dummies in their bed to mislead guards into thinking they had returned. The plot was discovered when a guard noticed one of the dummies during the evening count of inmates. On July 23, 1985, as officials at the State Penitentiary attempted to conduct a shakedown in C Building, known as Animal House, inmates set fire, flooded their cells, broke toilets, and used the broken porcelain to attack officers. They accused guards of beating them, chaining them to beds, using tear gas on them, and otherwise abusing them. The uprising continued for two days and resulted in the removal from their cells of metal furniture, some personal belongings, and even their clothes, leaving them in only their underwear until order could be restored. On August 6 the Richmond commonwealth attorney predicted continued violence at the State Penitentiary as a result of the fact that "state prison officials were so intent on clearing up problems at Mecklenburg Correctional Center that they had made [the State Penitentiary] a haven for hard-core convicts" (paraphrased, *NL*, August 8, 1985, p. 13). The next day an inmate was murdered at the State Penitentiary. As similar events continued at state prisons through the months, they began to be lost on back pages of the newspapers until November 27, 1985, when Lem Tuggle and three other inmates in the left side of C Pod of Building No. 1 of Mecklenburg's Death Row (the same area where the successful escape originated) tried to force a control room guard to open the gate by threatening him with a fake gun and a bomb. Although the guard believed the gun was real, he refused to cooperate and the inmates exploded their matchstick bomb,

Long Gone

cracking a plexiglass window of the control room. The guard called for help, and the insurgents surrendered.

It is important to note that the increased media attention to these escapes and uprisings resulted in a misleading perception of the prevalence of such problems. Indeed prison escapes during this period were far fewer than in prior years. While a decade before the escape, in 1974, prison escapes numbered 513 (or 87.2 per 1,000 inmates), in recent years escapes have generally been under one hundred, and most escapees have been minimum- or medium-custody convicts who simply walked away from work crews. During the 1984 fiscal year there were 108 escapes (11 per 1,000). Compared to the lowest number in recent years of 80 escapes in fiscal year 1978 (10.1 per 1,000), escapes during 1984 were certainly not appreciably increased. The most recent report shows that escapes are at an all-time low, escapes during the 1985 fiscal year dropping to 54 (or 5.2 per 1,000 inmates).[6].

Correctional personnel were unable to conceal their frustration in dealing with the problems of staff, discipline, and public image plaguing Virginia prisons as a result of the escape. In July 1984 the acting warden of Mecklenburg, Sherman Townley, pointed out that prisoners aware of the political pressures arising from the Mecklenburg escape and the threat to dismiss high ranking supervisors if disruptions continued were consequently motivated to provoke further disruptions. He predicted that it might be seven years before the prison system could return to normal because of the escape and the pressure from higher up (*NL*, July 12, 1984, p. 15). Following the August 1984 uprising a frustrated Landon declared that officials would do whatever was required to maintain control: "It's time to get tough. . . . I've just about had enough of Mecklenburg," he declared (*TD*, August 5, 1984, p. A-4).

Prison and correctional officials began to take a series of steps to control their populations, steps which ironically recall Virginia's 1831–32 "crackdown" on slaves following the Nat Turner revolt. Privileges were restricted, lockdowns, and shakedowns became commonplace, and, according to some inmates, abuse by guards increased:

"I Raised Hell While I Was There"

The guards took their resentment against us.... After the escape, the guards that you considered okay turned to cold assholes. They all felt the heat and they returned it to us.... Take Officer ———. He was once a decent guard. After the escape.... he was named Superior Officer of the newly instituted security force called 'TACT TEAM.' Their job is to dismember any violence that may occur here. He was responsible for several beatings, and made it known to all inmates that he wasn't going to take no shit. Recently he was sent to this old (and I mean old) man cell to get him. The old man refused to come out and Jackson went in and beat the hell out of the man.

Undated letter from prisoner at Mecklenburg,
written between March 15 and 19, 1985

Prison officials also enacted restrictions on visits of lawyers to Mecklenburg. On October 2, 1984, a U.S. district judge ordered them to discontinue those restrictions. Also in response to some of the restrictions imposed on inmates, on December 4 the ACLU again charged corrections officials with violating the 1983 class-action settlement. On December 18, 1984, Mecklenburg officials began monitoring the telephone calls of Death Row inmates. Despite the fact that the investigation into this situation revealed evidence of wrongdoing, the Mecklenburg County prosecutor refused to prosecute in the case, pointing out that those involved were either not aware that they were acting criminally or were overzealous in attempts to prevent another escape or were guilty of no more than bad judgment. On March 3, 1985, a class-action suit was filed on behalf of the Death Row inmates affected by the wiretapping, asking for $2.5 million in damages.

Meanwhile, a beseiged Robb administration was also taking every step possible to convince the public that something was being done. On June 7, 1984, that administration asked the state and federal courts to dismiss appeals of escapees, contending that they waived their right to appeal by breaking out of prison. On August 11 Robb issued a series of letters to express confidence in and boost the morale of prison guards and to explain to legislators steps being taken to deal with the problems in the prison system; he encouraged "everyone to help keep the lid on" and insisted that "whatever force is necessary" will be used to maintain order. Republicans responded that a lid should not be kept on solutions to the problems and that the Robb administration had "muzzled" Corrections Department personnel. They called for public hearings on the prison situation. On September 22 he made an unannounced inspectional visit to Mecklenburg Correctional Center and on December 10 to Nottoway prison. The unusual presence of high level officials at the Mecklenburg site was noted by an official at the penitentiary: "Before the escape, nobody ever came to Mecklenburg. Afterwards everyone converged on Mecklenburg. I looked out and saw the governor's helicopter landing on the grounds. Landon came—and White—and others" (Mecklenburg, February 28, 1985). In an interview during the first week of October, Franklin E. White, secretary of Transportation and Public Safety, declaring, "I can't imagine any crisis bigger than having six people walk out of death row," conceded that the crisis was "the biggest one" of Robb's term in office, but promised that he was reviewing proposals for improvement "with much greater sensitivity than I would ordinarily" (*TD*, October 7, 1984, p. 16). On November 30, 1984, the newly appointed Corrections Chief Sielaff announced that 132 new guards would be hired and the whole security system would be revamped. On December 26, 1984, Sielaff announced that some of Mecklenburg's most dangerous prisoners would be transferred to other prisons. On March 14, 1985, he announced a complete reorganization of the Corrections Department that would create fourteen new high ranking positions while eliminating twenty-four current ones. Among the offices affected by this reorganization were seven assistant directors, seven office managers, the head of the public information bureau, and the chief of operations for parole and probation. In an effort to improve the image of the Corrections Department, Seilaff also received the authorization of the State Board of Corrections to respond to public "fallacious" remarks by employees, even to provide reporters "case histories" of employees making critical remarks (*NL*, March 14, 1985, p. 13).

The ultimate step taken by the state to counter public criticism is seen by many to be the executions of the Brileys. Black prisoners were unanimous in the belief that those executions were expe-

"I Raised Hell While I Was There"

dited because their flight had caused the State of Virginia so much embarrassment. In the last conversation with his brother Linwood on the day of his death, Anthony Briley told him that "this is something they [prison officials] are doing to get the public off their back" (*NL*, October 13, 1985, p. 5). One Mecklenburg inmate wrote to me, "Most (inmates here) feel that the escape led to the embarrassment of the state so badly that the state executed the Briley brothers to calm the tension of society and take some of the heat off their ass for looking like a damn fool, for allowing six death row men to escape and not have any inside help" (March 14, 1985). A Death Row inmate confided to me that later evidence uncovered by investigators revealed that some of their earlier releases regarding the escape and the role of the Brileys contained misrepresentations, but that they did not want to admit that publicly; there were so many lies passed on to the media that in many instances the guards and other officials knew were lies, he continued, "but they don't want to back down and admit it or they have other reasons for preferring not to have the truth come out. They wanted to get rid of the Brileys, and they could use this as an excuse to expedite that goal" (telephone conversation, spring 1985). Five condemned men had been on Death Row longer than the Brileys, whose executions occurred less than five years after their sentencing; the average stay on Death Row, according to a Justice Department survey, is six to seven years (*TD*, October 14, 1984, p. D-2).

The new warden of Mecklenburg, Toni V. Bair, who took over on January 16, 1985, also set about to improve the image of Mecklenburg. He has attempted to achieve that goal by constantly reiterating what a "hellhole" it was when he first visited, suggesting that violence and mayhem were everyday occurrences, that trash fires burned all over the institution when he arrived, a building was flooded, and the inmates were "screaming and cursing and ranting and raving." He was informed, he suggests, that such behavior happened "all the time" (*TD*, May 26, 1985, p. 1; similar comments appear in the *Post*, May 28, 1985, p. A-8). He contrasts that dramatically depicted image with what he portrays as order and control and warm interactions between prison personnel and inmates since his arrival. This contrast is illustrated during carefully orchestrated press visits to the institution, the goal of which is to display and have publicized an effectively operating prison with inmates receiving humane treatment. The Grand July investigating the April 19 uprising at the Virginia State Penitentiary noted "the cosmetic nature of Mecklenburg's limitations has even reached the comic proportions of shipping out unruly inmates at press and media visitation time" (*NL*, August 20, 1985, p. 1). Later that same special Grand Jury noted that "not only were inmates moved out, but cosmetic inmates [disabled inmates with low I.Q.s and docile personalities] were moved in, and, then, after media days, were removed" (*NL*, October 10, 1985, p. 3). Bair's carefully controlled image is steadfastly protected by efforts to control commentaries from within the institution, both by employees and inmates. The efforts to create the new image include such hypes as focusing in interviews on a softball team of guards sporting Great Escape T-shirts playing against a team of inmates and enjoying a barbecue together— the message—guards and inmates who were before Bair came throwing feces and punches at each other are now tossing balls in the friendly all-American game, while the escape has become a historical event that they can all share. While the warden points out to his select visitors examples of freshly painted cells and happy prisoners watching soap operas and intoning how good things are since Bair, some prisoners express amusement at the extensive media play: "We're getting more press coverage than Nancy Reagan," quips one (*TD*, May 30, 1985, p. B-10), and others insist that the changes are "cosmetic" or "were only to put on a good face for the press and TV" (*TD*, May 30, 1985, p. B-10). What seeps out through the cracks of Bair's effective media blitz are the almost effectively silenced complaints that everything must be done Bair's way (*TD*, May 26, 1985, p. A-4). Furthermore, wardens from other institutions complain, Bair has been able to create the image of tremendous improvements because he has been provided increased personnel and funding for improved programs,

"I Raised Hell While I Was There"

and he has been allowed to ship out his problem inmates. One warden, quoted in the *Times Dispatch*, insisted, "[Mecklenburg's] been turned into a kiddy farm and many inmate troublemakers have been sent to Powhatan and the State Penitentiary to cause trouble there. It's another political situation. Hell, any warden who's given extra money and staff could do the same job" (May 26, 1985, p. 1). His complaint is reinforced by an inmate at the State Penitentiary who noted that C Building of the State Penitentiary and M Building of the Powhatan Correctional Center, maximum security units at the two institutions, are "the new Mecklenburg" (*NL*, May 6, 1985, p. 1),[7] by Richmond Commonwealth Attorney Aubrey M. David in his previously quoted statement; and by the findings of the Grand Jury investigating the April 18 uprising at the Virginia State Penitentiary, who accused that several of the inmates transferred from Mecklenburg, which was specifically designed to handle such prisoners, to the State Penitentiary, were returned to Mecklenburg, but within two days they had been sent back to the State Penitentiary. That Grand Jury directly attributed the problem at the State Penitentiary to those transfers.

Bair's promotional campaign includes his own image as well. He goes to great lengths to project himself as being different from run of the mill prison wardens—refined, cultured, and accustomed to the good life. He casually lets it be known that he reflected on the decision to come to Virginia while in his outdoor hot tub, that he goes about the sometimes dirty work of interacting with prisoners while "I'm wearing a $500 suit and a $1000 cashmere coat." He brags about attending the ballet, the theater, and art auctions and not fitting the typical image of a warden— "Some have called me 'The Renaissance Man'" (*Post*, May 28, 1985, p. A-8).

Local jail authorities have been vociforously complaining for several months that the state prison system is refusing to take state prisoners out of local jails, thereby forcing them to do their work and maintain prisoners that they should not have to continue to house and are not equipped to deal with. The Henrico

Long Gone

sheriff accused, "They've been under a lot of fire and I think
they're trying to relieve pressure by transferring the problem to local jails" (*TD*, February 12, 1985, p. 3). In August 1985 that battle still raged with the state's 125 sheriffs, most of them Democrats, demanding some action from the Robb administration, as the Republicans capitalized on the attacks in the heated gubernatorial campaign. The chief spokesman for the Republican gubernatorial nominee assured that his candidate would provide improved leadership in that area. The indirect relationship between this controversy and the Briley debacle was ironically highlighted when on August 15, 1985, Channel 6 reported that over the weekend a mini-riot in the women's section of the Richmond jail, which required the use of two cannisters of tear gas to retain control, was begun when the woman who had offered testimony in James Briley's appeal on the day of his death refused to turn off her radio. She had been convicted of perjury in a trial stemming from that appeal, but had not been transferred to the state prison system. As the cameras focused on numerous women packed in crowded cells, one yelled, "She won't suppose to be here noway! She was supposed to be in a State prison!" Finally on August 19 the Robb administration announced that it was spending close to $4 million to make room in state prisons for 500 inmates from overcrowded local jails. Immediately, state prison officials began protesting that the shift would exacerbate overcrowding and violence in state prisons. That every step taken to correct one condition regarding the state penal system since the Great Escape has provoked criticism that it has caused another problem has led the *Times Dispatch* to label the dilemma Sielaff's law (editorial, August 22, 1985, p. A-13).

The escape served also to revive the debate about the location of the prison within the Mecklenburg community. Despite the fact that the prison was an economic boon, providing employment in the area, there has always been widespread opposition to it. After the escape the community was so appalled at their association with the Correctional Center that one person told me there was a move to change their name from Mecklenburg in

"I Raised Hell While I Was There"

order to disassociate themselves from the prison; the move was sparked by the fact that the very mention of Mecklenburg was having an adverse effect on tourism in the area (Mecklenburg, February 28, 1985).

Thus, while prison guards were taunted and disciplined for their blunders, while FBI and local police agents were following bogus leads, while prison officials were receiving dressing downs for continued disruptions, while courts were knocking down restrictions imposed by prison authorities, and while top government officials were trying to salvage their political careers, there were those who characteristically found the chaos and confusion of such authority figures amusing. Powerful men who wield awesome power, who daily determine when—or if—others will eat, shower, sleep, play, or die, were literally and figuratively left with their pants down by those insignificant others, and in the chaos that followed they didn't seem able to begin to regain their dignity and control. One Death Row inmate quipped, "I just thought it was funny when the takeover began. . . . Laughter is our only form of retaliation." He also laughed as he recalled the ineffective shakedowns before the escapes conducted by authorities unable to find weapons with a map of their location and unable to foil an escape that they possessed full information about. He insisted that the escapees did not need outside help because "The officials just weren't smart enought to stop them" (*TD*, July 15, 1984, pp. 1, 17). One Black guard at Mecklenburg told me, "While my mother and most of the older people were scared to death, my young brothers enjoyed making fun of the police officers because the Brileys were outsmarting them. When we passed a blockade just across the North Carolina line, he jeered, 'Hey, didn't anybody tell you they [the Brileys] were in Philadelphia?' " (February 28, 1985).

That six condemned men could possibly affect the geography of the state (if the name of Mecklenburg is changed), the design, operation, and staffing of the entire prison system, the upcoming gubernatorial elections, the prospects of a presidential hopeful (Robb is frequently regarded as a future presidential candidate),

Long Gone

and the careers of countless officials from the prison guards to cabinet members, was indeed a wild and ludicrous joke. Thus, however relieved the community might have been that the Brileys had had their wings taken away from them, that they were back behind bars, there was also an amused acknowledgement that they sure tore up "heaven" and raised hell while they were flying.

"I Raised Hell While I Was There"

CHAPTER 7

"Walkin' to the 'Lectric Chair"

The Execution of the Brileys

I'm walkin' to the 'lectric chair,
　　with a preacher by my side,
I'm walkin' to the 'lectric chair,
　　with a preacher by my side,
It got me for cold-blooded murder
　　and the truth can't be denied.

Song sung by Blue Boy in 1929,
from *Blues Fell This Morning*, p. 225

　　When the Braileys were captured and returned to Virginia, they were taken directly to the basement of A Building in the State Penitentiary in Richmond, where all executions take place. They were greeted upon their arrival at about 9:15 P.M. on June 21, 1984, with widespread cheering from the inmates. Initially some reporters questioned whether or not the prisoners were cheering or jeering, but numerous inmates informed me that they were indeed cheering, acclaiming their feat of escaping. Now that the Brileys were physically closer to Virginia's electric chair, none doubted the imminence of their deaths. After a moratorium of twenty years, five months, and one week, Virginia had on August 10, 1982, executed one man, Frank J. Coppola, a white former policeman who had chosen to forego appeals. If a white man had been executed, even one who had decided not to fight his execution, there was no doubt that many Black men would die, especially two who had defied and embarrassed the system by escaping. Capital punishment from its early days in Virginia had been a tool for repressing slave rebellion and has always fallen disproportionately on the heads of Black men.

From their beginnings in this country Afro-Americans were accused of "inherent criminality." Terms such as "lawless," "monsters," "wretches," "fiends," and "savages" were constantly applied to them. Blacks are referred to as "people of such base and corrupt natures" in a 1732 Virginia law prohibiting their serving as witnesses in trials.[1] The application of such accusations was, as Philip J. Schwarz notes, "more than a crude, racist smear. It was also an integral part of the Europeans' ideology of domination, with which they justified, not just excused the denial of many English rights to slaves taken from Africa."[2] Obviously a person who had no basic human qualities also required more extreme repressive measures to protect civilization from his savagery. Any rebellion of a Black against the system that repressed and enslaved him was viewed by the larger society as an evil act, and all of its power was brought to bear to repress the "bad" niggers who protested. The most extreme laws were implemented in Virginia and other Southern states to punish and indeed get rid of any dangerous slaves—and dangerous slaves were those who defied their masters, resisted enslavement, or attempted to escape. As a matter of course, punishment for Negroes accused of certain crimes was more extreme than that for whites. A review of laws passed in Virginia reflects an obsession with the problem of runaways. Innumerable laws, acts, and resolutions were passed to fix punishment for slaves who ran away or conspired to run away and of whites or free Blacks who conspired with them or assisted them; to provide compensation to the owners of slaves who escaped from jail; to provide rewards to any who assisted in the capture and return of runaways (these included a cash reward and often mileage expenses for returning the slave); and to prevent the citizens of other states (especially New York) from carrying away Virginia slaves. Laws were passed providing that Negroes who ran away, resisted arrest, resisted their master, conspired to rebel, raped, or committed a third offense of stealing be killed, and sometimes this sentence included dismemberment. Incidents are recorded of Blacks whose bodies were decapitated

Richmond County judge ordered a slave's body to be quartered and displayed at different locations in the county. George M. Stroud lists sixty-odd offenses for which Black slaves exclusively were liable for execution. Schwarz points out that "every single slave convicted of being the principal in a case of killing a white [in Virginia] between 1706 and 1739 was sentenced to hang."[3] Slaves sentenced to be executed sometimes had their sentences commuted to deportation, often as an economic exigency occasioned by the expense of compensating owners for the loss of such valuable property were the slaves executed. One 1691 law cited by Guild provides, "The [runaways] may be killed or destroyed by gun or otherwise whatsoever, *provided that the owner of any slave killed shall be paid four thousand pounds of tobacco by the public* (p. 47: italics mine). Numerous laws and acts specified restitution to be made to the owner for the loss of his slave property, and in numerous instances owners were paid as much as two or three thousand dollars for their loss. No mention is made in any of these laws about restitution to widows or widowers or children for suffering any loss deserving compensation. Clearly the life of the Black man or woman had no value except in terms of his or her worth to the owner. This paradoxical situation, highlighted by Virginia's paying a lawyer $10.00 to defend Nat Turner and paying his owner's estate $375 for the loss it suffered because of his execution, finds its present-day parallels in the amount of money paid by the State of Virginia to defend indigents facing capital punishment.

One of the most severe punishments awaited the slave convicted of abducting, raping, or attempting to ravish a white woman. For such an offense he might be castrated or executed. A free Black would also be executed for the same charges. Extreme punishment was also decreed for the Negro found guilty of other crimes, such as robbery, carrying a weapon, leaving his owner's plantation without a certificate, or being found on a boat. Punishment for such offenses included imprisonment, deportation, "lashes on the bare back, well laid on," fines, confiscation of property, having his ear nailed to the pillory and then cut off,

"Walkin' to the 'Lectric Chair"

and being "burnt in the hands in open court" (Guild, p. 154). Laws made clear that there was to be no punishment or responsibility incurred if the offending slave "shall *happen* to die by means of dismembering by court order, or by any stroke or blow during his or her correction by his or her owner" (Guild, p. 153, italics mine). Free Blacks were vulnerable to a variety of offenses that did not affect whites and could face a series of serious punishments for not registering, being found without their free papers, carrying weapons, being vagrants (not having a job), piloting a boat, trading with slaves, preaching, holding meetings, selling or giving away liquor, seeking an education, instructing other Blacks, writing or circulating a book, returning to the state after going to a nonslaveholding state, owning dogs, and gambling. Such offenses could result in imprisonment, beatings, transportation, death, or sale into slavery. Although laws in Virginia regarding Blacks were constantly revised and repealed, the severity of these laws remained a constant.

It is also interesting to note that the tenor of earlier laws clearly reflects a rule that by practice, if not by law, remains in effect to the present day—that acts by whites against Blacks shall not be regarded as serious offenses. Several pre-Civil War laws in Virginia treat Black victims of white violence as victims of accidental rather than intentional actions. Thus a 1669 Virginia law states, "If a slave resist his master and by the *extremity of the correction, chance to die*, his death shall not be a felony" (Guild, p. 43; italics mine). By 1705 the law exonerated the white in even clearer terms: "If any slave resist his master, or owner, *or other person*, by his or her order correcting such slave, and *shall happen to be killed in such correction*, it shall not be accounted felony; but the master, owner, and every such other person so giving correction shall be free and acquit of all punishment and accusation for the same, *as if such incident had never happened*" (Guild, pp. 152–53; italics mine). By 1723 no excuse, such as the fact that a slave was resisting, was required to absolve any white who committed a violent act against him; the law decreed that no person "indicted for the murder of any slave . . . [shall] incur any punishment for the offense or *misfortune*" (Guild, p. 154; italics mine). The precedent established

Long Gone

by these seventeenth and eighteenth century laws continues to manifest itself in the treatment of crime by Blacks against whites and vice versa in Virginia and other Southern states today, where all studies show that the most serious crime remains the murder of a white person by a Black man. Clearly the three classes of homicides that Raymond Fosdick observed in Southern police departments in a study he published in 1920 still remains all too applicable today: one police officer explained those three classes to him: "If a nigger kills a white man, that's murder. If a white man kills a nigger, that's justifiable homicide. If a nigger kills another nigger, that's one less nigger."[4] A study of nineteen death penalty cases in Virginia since 1977, cited in a petition appealing a death penalty in the state recently, revealed that a Black man who kills a white person has an 8.2 percent chance of being sentenced to death; a white man who kills a white person has a 1.3 percent chance of being sentenced to death; and a Black who kills another Black has only a 0.6 percent chance of being sentenced to death. No white person convicted of killing a Black received a death penalty (TD, May 14, 1985 p. A-14). Of the twenty-six men on Virginia's Death Row in August 1984, twenty-one were convicted of murdering white victims (NL, August 25, 1984). Blacks are convinced that some of the small percentage of Blacks, such as James Briley, who are sentenced to death for the murders of other Blacks received those sentences because authorities were convinced they had murdered whites but could not develop a case for a capital conviction. Indeed James Briley appears to be the only person executed in Virginia during the last two centuries for killing a Black person.[5] A study of the executions in Virginia from 1908, when the state took over executions from the localities and began electrocuting condemned felons (one felon was hanged under local authority in 1909), to 1982, reveals that only 34 of the 238 executed were white, and the 33 whites for whom the crimes are indicated were all executed for murder. Of the 204 Blacks executed, 130 were executed for murder; 13 for attempted rape; 40 for rape; 6 for robbery; and 1 for rape and robbery; the offense is not listed for 14 Blacks. The one female was a Black woman executed in 1912 for murder (figures based

"Walkin' to the 'Lectric Chair"

upon William J. Bowers' listing of executions in Virginia from 1908-82, which includes Frank J. Coppola, the first post-Furman execution in Virginia and the only white among the four post-Furman executions in the state, as well as the only one who chose not to appeal).[6] When one considers the above figures of the executions of a disproportionate number of Blacks almost exclusively for the murders, rapes, and robberies of whites in light of the fact that Blacks are murdered at a much higher rate than whites, the disparity becomes even more blatant. National statistics indicate that a Black man's chance of being killed is one out of twenty-one, while the risk of Americans overall is one out of 133 (JET, May 27, 1985, p. 37). In Richmond only nineteen of this year's ninety-four murder victims were white (sixty-four were Black males; ten were Black females; ten were white males; nine were white females; and one was an Asian male. Of the sixty-four Black males killed, twenty-seven were twenty-five years old or younger).[7]

In similar manner the grave offense of rape committed by a Black man against a white woman has rarely been treated as an offense at all when the races of the perpetrator and victim were reversed. Schwarz observes that "No eighteenth-century Virginia court whose records have survived ever convicted a slave of raping another slave or a white man of raping a female slave." Indeed, during this period no court even heard a case "against any white man for violating the common law of rape when the victim was a slave. . . . The law simply did not criminalize the rape of slave women" (pp. 143, 147).

Study after study reveals the disproportionate number of Blacks sentenced to death and longer prison terms than their white counterparts found guilty of murder and rape. This situation becomes even more iniquitous when one considers that those Blacks receiving stiffer penalties were also less likely than their white counterparts to have had equally efficient legal assistance or to have faced an unbiased jury and judge. Bowers cites studies showing that Blacks "were *indicted, charged, convicted, and sentenced* to death in disproportionate numbers—indicating that the full extent of racial discrimination will not be revealed in an

Long Gone

analysis of any single stage in the justice process. Also by taking the victim's as well as the offender's race into account, these investigations turned up consistent evidence that discrimination throughout the justice process was especially concentrated against blacks whose victims were whites" (p. 69; italics mine). These studies also clearly indicate that the harsher sentences meted out to Blacks remain a Southern phenomenon. Executions for rape have been almost exclusively limited to the South and to Blacks convicted of raping whites. Since 1908, though 55 percent of those imprisoned for rape in Virginia have been Black, 100 percent of those executed for rape have been Black.[8] Furthermore, though Blacks constitute less than 20 percent of the population of Virginia, more than half of the prison population of the penal institutions in the state is Black. The blatantly discriminatory nature of capital punishment was one of the major causes leading to the temporary suspension of executions in this country as a result of the June 29, 1972, *Furman vs. Georgia* ruling. Some states that wished to maintain capital punishment, such as Virginia, responded by revising their laws to establish two types of capital punishment laws: " 'mandatory' statutes, making the death penalty automatic upon conviction for specifically defined capital offenses; and 'guided discretion' statutes, providing guidelines for sentencing in the form of explicitly enumerated aggravating and mitigating circumstances."[9] Virginia's new capital murder statute was enacted in 1977. Currently thirty-seven states have capital punishment, but only twelve of them have carried out executions since the Furman moratorium. All except three of the forty-six executions that had been carried out by July 1985 took place in the South (the exceptions were Utah, Nevada, and Indiana).[10] Looking over the history of capital punishment in Virginia and Alabama through July 1985, Watt Espy, in the report of his Capital Punishment Research Project, June 26, 1985, noted, "Certainly in these states, a distinct pattern of racial discrimination in the application of the death penalty is established—a pattern that, to say the very least, borders to some extent, on a policy of genocide."

The inequities suffered by Blacks in Southern courts have been

"Walkin' to the 'Lectric Chair"

the subject of innumerable items in Black folklore. The situation has been most succinctly expressed by two proverbs: "Cockroach nebber git justice when chicken judge," and "When all the judges is foxes, ain't much justice for a poor goose." Another verse from a folksong captures the essence of the previous discussion: "If a white man kills a Negro, they hardly carry it to court / If a Negro kills a white man, they hang him like a goat."[11] In one tale, a Black defendant, recognizing the disparity in the weight given to testimony by whites and Blacks, asks the judge to give him a white witness rather than to appoint a lawyer. In another tale a white man who has received a death penalty retorts to a Negro who has also received the same penalty and who calmly accepts his punishment and encourages the white man to do the same, "Yeah, you kin talk [about the crimes we did to deserve this punishment]. YAWL used to it!" (S&J, p. 172). In other tales white Klansmen order the judge to hurry up with the trial so they can hang the Black defendant; and a white motorist who has run into Black pedestrians is assured by the policeman that he has no need to fear that *he* will face any charges: "Those Negroes are obviously at fault; the one who has been knocked into your car will be charged with illegal entry and the one who has been knocked several feet away will be charged with leaving the scene of the accident."

Whether the Black victim of the system complains, "They had me arrested for murder / and I never harmed a man"[12] or admits "I'm walkin' to the 'lectric chair, with a preacher by my side, / It got me for cold-blooded murder and the truth can't be denied" (*Blues Fell This Morning*, p. 225), the implication inherent in Black folklore is that Black people have been victimized by a court system which denied them a fair trial and accords them a stiffer penalty. As Ben Chavis recently put it: "The criminal justice system is appropriately named—it is a criminal system. That system condones the criminal conduct of the rich and powerful while crushing and dehumanizing the disproportionately high numbers of Blacks, the poor, the weak and the damned who get caught up in its vicious cycle."[13]

Long Gone

Current events in a most disturbing manner reinforce the fact that, as during slavery when the runaway slave was characterized as a thief and his master as a victim, the same elements of American society still too often ironically serve in diverse ways to victimize the Black citizen and then declare him the villain. The precedent lies in the "sacred" right the slaveholders of Virginia and the rest of the South claimed to maintain and protect their "property."[14] In resolutions protesting the protection of fugitive slaves by Northern states, Virginia complained, "Could the men . . . agree that the felon who should steal from a master might go acquit," and noted, "It is the pride and glory of our country to be an asylum for the persecuted and the oppressed of every nation, but should any state erect herself into a place of refuge for thieves and robbers, she would sully that glory" (Guild, pp. 201–202).

Such arrogant characterization of the enslaver as right and virtuous and of the enslaved as thief and villain reflects some of the same racist tendency to ipso facto judge white as right and Black as guilty manifested in the highly publicized Bernard Hugo Goetz shooting in the subway of New York City. Public reactions quickly conceded the white man who felt threatened the right to shoot down four Black boys who asked him for $5.00, two of them in the back, leaving one paralyzed and comatose. He reportedly looked at one felled by an earlier bullet and seeing no blood said, "You don't look too bad, here's another," whereupon he shot him again (*Newsweek*, March 11, 1985, p. 50). The Black boys were quickly described as "menacing," "criminals," "punks," and the man who pumped at least five bullets into their bodies was described as the victim. The antebellum "rights" of the white man seemed to many to be all too willingly conceded here. Even as balanced judgments consider the possible terror felt by a previously mobbed man who may have been convinced that he was in real danger of attack; even as they concede the possibility that those four Black boys were intending to use their undrawn, pocketed weapons and to rob Goetz; they must realize also that such quick reaching of judgments and dispensing of punishment

"Walkin' to the 'Lectric Chair"

would hardly have been considered justifiably if the races of the "victim" and "assailants" were switched, for then it would have no historical precedent.

Given, therefore, the continuing historical reality in which the drama of the Brileys was played out, the question of guilt or innocence of the crimes of which they were accused was only one concern for many viewers; suspicions that they might have been judged and prosecuted on the basis of long standing racist assumptions were aroused. The recognition that they could not afford competent legal counsel was clear. Virginia's court-appointed lawyers are among the poorest paid in the nation, their payment for a capital murder trial before July 1984 being $572. Furthermore the state does not, as a matter of course, provide lawyers for appeals for a person sentenced to death after his conviction is upheld by the State Supreme Court. Thus convicts such as the Brileys frequently have to rely upon the service of volunteer laywers. The lawyer who represented Linwood Briley through a long series of appeals received payment of only $20.00 for services which she valued at $50,000 (*NL*, June 27, 1985, p. 4; *NL*, October 16, 1984, p. 6). She also had to endure derision for her defense of Briley; one writer began a letter to her, "Dear Nigger Lover" (*NL*, October 16, 1984, p. 6).

Even the question of the guilt of the Brileys was not one conceded by some people familiar with them and with the case, some of whom, like Linwood Briley's lawyer, noted the common tendency to portray a monstrous image of them in order to justify their destruction: "It's easier to execute a monster," the lawyer contended (*NL*, October 16, 1984, p. 6). In the one press conference that each of the brothers gave shortly before their deaths, both expressed concern about and tried to counteract the vicious images of them that had been popularized. Linwood Briley complained, "They blew me up like some robotic monster" (*TD*, September 30, 1984, p. A-4), and James Briley insisted, "I was NOT this animal that the press had made me out to be or the justice department had made me out to be" (press conference, April 16, 1985).

The brothers themselves consistently maintained their inno-

Long Gone

cence until their deaths. Some friends of theirs prior to the killing and some, like Reverend Odie Brown, who met them later, considered it preposterous that they could have committed such heinous crimes. One inmate at the State Penitentiary who had been a close friend of the Brileys as long as he could remember says Linwood denied the killings to him, and he is convinced he would not have denied it to such a close confidant as himself had he been guilty (November 26, 1984). Several inmates questioned certain evidence that had contributed to the conviction of the brothers. In a big group with whom I spoke at the State Penitentiary on November 26, 1984, there was general consensus that it was ludicrous to have convicted them largely on the testimony of a confessed murderer, who could be expected to say anything to protect himself. Others in this group and elsewhere found it unlikely that intelligent men like the Brileys would have committed three murders when they knew they were being tailed and that the police were right outside the apartment.[15] Others expressed amazement that if the police were actually present that night they would not have responded upon hearing a gunshot and seeing men whom they already suspected of prior murders come out with a rifle.

Others tended to doubt the Brileys' guilt simply because they were cynical about the justice system, having themselves been victimized by it, many contended. One proclaimed, "It is not fair, it ain't never been fair, and it ain't never going to be fair" (November 26, 1984).

Whether inmates questioned their guilt or accepted their "possible" guilt, a major concern of many was that the execution of Linwood Briley had set a dangerous precedent whereby the state of Virginia would once again begin executing Black men, something they considered a modern form of lynching. Of course, for several the die had been cast with the execution of Coppola, who was white: one inmate proclaimed, "Make no mistake about it — five Black dudes are going to die because of that one white guy who asked to die. If they fry one of their own kind, you know what they'll do to us. That's just opening up the door" (Virginia State Penitentiary, November 26, 1984). In an earlier conversation

"Walkin' to the 'Lectric Chair"

prior to Linwood Briley's execution, one inmate had asserted that whatever you think of the Brileys, "If they fry one nigger, they'll fry others" (Virginia State Penitentiary, August 6, 1984). One inmate during the November 26 conversation exclaimed, "They didn't prove him [Linwood] guilty," and another insisted, "We don't know anything about who killed whom [of those victims

Long Gone

Linwood Briley (left) and James Briley (above) during press conferences at the Virginia State Penitentiary. Grateful acknowledgment is made to Richmond Newspapers, Inc., for permission to use these photographs.

for whose murders the Brileys were convicted], but we do know who killed Linwood Briley—we know that for damn sure!"

The guilt of society is something that is frequently noted in conversations with these inmates about the death penalty. Many of them see themselves (and in many instances justifiably so, though clearly there are also those who use this as a rationalization for whatever offenses they committed) as victims of a racist and violent society, and they are angry that they must pay such a high price for the crimes they committed or were accused of committing while other extreme acts of violence are condoned by society or excused or less severely punished. One prison bard concludes a poem on the escape:

"Walkin' to the 'Lectric Chair"

But as the switch is set and all the circuits are set,
I wonder if they're guilty of the charges they've met.
And if so, they're only reflecting society's flow—
A hundred and eighteen thousand in Hiroshima,
A land once inhabited by Indians,
Gunsmoke, rifleman, viciousness is the way they go.

Charles Satchell, Virginia State
Penitentiary, August 6, 1984

Another poem by an inmate at the Virginia State Penitentiary addresses itself to "Men of Death Row," characterizes them as suffering the worst penalty of being "damned from birth," and asserts that they are being murdered to "silence [the] fear" of this mighty nation. In numerous conversations and poems, and in some written statements collected by inmate Emmett O. Johnson, Jr., prisoners employ a variety of terms when referring to the state of Virginia as executioner: "depraved," "society's sophisticated psychopaths," "blood-thirsty vampires," "wolves," "merciless killers," "assasins," "cold-blooded," "butchers," "a Mafia-type execution. Dial a hit."[16] One prisoner suggested that the slogan for the state should be changed from "Virginia is for lovers" to "Virginia is for murderers."

Conversely, many of these same inmates see the Brileys (and other who have been executed) as victims. One poet typically described Linwood Briley as "young, black, . . . sacrificial, . . . oppressed, . . . a lamb for slaughter" (Larry Batten, "Briley: They Know Not What They Do," Mecklenburg Correctional Center, March 25, 1985).

Despite the lawyers' court appeals, requests for a stay of execution, and appeals to the governor for clemency, despite the protests and appeals of numerous groups and individuals, including a group of Black ministers, the Virginia Civil Liberties Union, and the NAACP (one of the latest groups to register a protest [on October 5, 1985], seemingly because some members were reluctant to save the Brileys because of the heinous nature of their crimes and because of their escape), and despite the public appeals of the two condemned men, the shadow of Virginia's oaken electric chair daily loomed more ominously over the heads

Long Gone

of the Briley brothers. James had been transferred back to Mecklenburg on July 31, 1984, but Linwood, whose execution date was more imminent, remained at the Virginia State Penitentiary on Death Row, where some inmates insist the smell of burning flesh is a constant, even during the years when there were no electrocutions, and where they say the lights blink and you can hear clicking when the electric chair is cut on and off during testing.

On August 2, 1984, Linwood Briley, who was scheduled to be executed on August 17, was baptized by Reverend Odie Brown. On August 8, 1984, he received a stay of execution pending further order of the court, leaving open the possibility that he might still be executed as scheduled. The state proceeded with its plans to execute until August 17, when a postponement was announced just minutes prior to the beginning of the thirteen hour death watch. Later Linwood Briley was to comment that the guards seemed intent upon going on with the plans for his execution, despite the fact that his attorneys had informed him of the stay. When they realized the execution was off, they seemed depressed and disappointed, he added (press conference, September 29, 1984). On October 9 Briley lost appeals in the 4th U.S. Circuit Court of Appeals and in the U. S. Supreme Court (Justices Thurgood Marshall and William J. Brennan, Jr., dissented).

> I thought, maybe a reprieve, maybe good news.
> Maybe the electric chair blew a fuse.
>
> From "Death Row," *The Life*, p. 119

His new execution date was set for October 13, 1984.

Even as the frantic last-minute efforts went on to save his life, Linwood Briley retained his hope and his sense of humor. Reverend Brown told me, "I don't think Linwood thought he was going to be executed—not until the last minute" (interview, June 17, 1985), and a poem written by his brother James after the execution suggests that even five hours before his execution he still spoke of it in the conditional.

As October 13 unrelentingly approached, restlessness among the inmates in Virginia prisons increased and lockdowns became commonplace. At Mecklenburg on October 12, nineteen of the

"Walkin' to the 'Lectric Chair"

twenty-one inmates on Death Row protested the execution by signing a statement asking that they not be served meals "as a means of our peaceful protest of the execution of Linwood Briley by the people of the state and the 'so-called' legal system of our civilized society" (TD, October 13, 1984, p. A-8; the acting warden reported, however, that eleven of the signers of the notes did eat their meals). At the State Penitentiary on the day of the execution and the day after, about 350 inmates wore black arm bands to express their protest. Some who wished to participate in this quiet demonstration were afraid to do so, however, especially those who were coming up for parole (conversation, State Penitentiary, November 26, 1984).

Several controversies arose concerning the execution, one of which was the debate over who would witness it. Sgt. Norman A. Harding, the Richmond detective who headed the investigation that led to Briley's murder conviction, publicly expressed his disappointment that he was not selected to be one of the eight who, from a glass-enclosed area, would witness Linwood Briley's demise: "The main thing is seeing justice through to the end. . . . I was the one that started with him" (NL, October 4, 1984, p. 15). Bishop Walter F. Sullivan, who had initially been scheduled to be a witness, withdrew when Linwood suggested to him that his "presence at an execution was cooperation in an evil" (TD, October 9, 1984, p. B-8). On the night of the execution Bishop Sullivan spoke at a worship service where he thanked Briley for bringing the religious community together and for sparing him "the horror of witnessing his execution" (NL, October 13, 1984, p. 5), a statement that provoked quite a bitter and lengthy public furor in the community.

On the night of the execution a Richmond lawyer chosen as one of the witnesses reportedly left a recorded message on his home telephone: "I have gone down to the Spring Street hotel to see Mr. Briley, who could not do without me this evening" (TD, October 1, 1984, pp. 1 and 8).

On the morning of October 13 preparations of the prisoner for execution were begun, including the shaving of his head. That afternoon Briley saw his illegitimate son, who learned who his father was only after Briley was recaptured some four months before his death and who visited him several times during his last months. The ten-year old boy lamented that he was never allowed to touch his father: "If they'd let me, I'd give him a big hug and be real happy," he commented shortly before his father's death (*TD*, October 14, 1984, p. D-1). He went with his mother to say a tearful goodbye to his father through a glass partition on the afternoon of his execution.[17] Briley was also visited by his grandfather, two aunts, his brother from North Carolina, and Marie Deans, a prison reform activist. His mother, who had requested to be allowed to hug her son, was permitted a contact visit of about 45 minutes. His lawyer was also granted a contact visit, which she cut short because of the obvious discomfort the handcuffs were causing him.

At 5:55 Linwood talked on the telephone with his brother James. That night James wrote a poem about his brother's execution and their conversation, one verse of which read:

> I spoke to my brother at 5:55 P.M. on October 12th
> He was holding real strong
> even though he was being done wrong—
> He told me he love—love me which I already knew,
> but to hear it straight from him it was really something
>   new. . . .
> I ask what could I do to help him make it through—
> He ask me to remain strong and never give-up the fight
> If he should go down this cold dreary night.
>
> From "Linwood," in *FYSK Magazine*,
> 13 (Winter 1984), p. 18

At 6:15 Linwood talked on the telephone to his brother Anthony for seventeen minutes. Anthony, who cried during their conversation, frequently told Linwood he loved him (*NL*, October 13, 1984, p. 5).

Linwood did not order a special last meal, indicating that he would have whatever the other inmates were being served; prison

"Walkin' to the 'Lectric Chair"

officials decided that he should have a special meal, however, and he was served steak, a baked potato, green peas, a tossed salad, peaches, cake, punch and milk.

Reverend Odie Brown and Reverend Marjorie Bailey spent much of that last evening with Linwood Briley. He prepared for his execution with as much care as he might have prepared for a party, Reverend Brown told me, but he still couldn't believe that this was really happening. He kept repeating, "This is unbelievable. This is unbelievable." About 9:30 Linwood asked the chaplains to leave so that he could speak privately with his family on the telephone. When the chaplains returned about 10:40 P.M., Linwood Briley had been placed in a new cell; he had watched as all of his belongings from his other cell were packed and moved.[18] The chaplains found Linwood sitting in his new cell reading the Bible, a light falling over him creating a picturesque and symbolic tableau. A ballgame was on the hall TV, just outside his cell, but his concentration was all on the Bible. A guard came in and moved the hands on the big wall clock on his cell wall up two minutes, a cruel theft of precious time from a condemned man with less than twenty minutes of life remaining.[19] Less than ten minutes before his execution, Linwood said thank you to Reverend Brown (he never really told him goodbye) and asked him if he had a pen. Reverend Brown gave him a pen, and he sat down and wrote a note (see page 134).

This letter, written in a remarkably composed and steady hand, contains a challenging ambiguity which the writer probably intended. Our initial assumption that it is GOD that still lives on is challenged by the fact that "U-ME,-HE 'God' " are all on one line, perhaps suggesting that all of us live on; note also that "U-ME,-HE" are joined in such a way that God could be the synonym for *HE* or the synonym for all of us. Finally, "Still lives on" appears as the complimentary close in the letter, which could suggest that it refers to Linwood Briley. His last message was thus as much of an enigma as the man himself. When he finished his missive, Briley calmly handed the epistle to Reverend Brown. He demanded from the guards a watch and a ring that had been taken

Long Gone

from him, gave them to Reverend Bailey, and requested that they be given to his mother.

Briley's lawyer, who had worked until the last minute in a futile effort to secure a clemency appeal, rushed to the prison to witness the execution. She wanted to be sure that if the chair failed, he was set free (*NL*, October 26, 1984, p. 6). Reverend Brown later told me that when she came in she lamented, "I know he was innocent, but I can't prove it."

> "I'm walkin' to the 'lectric chair,
>   with a preacher by my side,
> I'm walkin' to the 'lectric chair,
>   with a preacher by my side."

Reverend Brown asked Linwood if he needed help in walking to his execution. He told the chaplains, "I can make it, but I want you to walk with me." One witness described Briley as nervous and trembling, but most other witnesses said he was calm and composed as, with his eyes closed, he walked the forty feet from his cell to the electric chair at approximately 10:55 P.M. Reverend Brown told me, "When the warden read his execution order to him and asked him if he had anything to say, he said [calmly and softly], 'I'm innocent.' And when he sat in the chair, he adjusted himself as if to cause them no difficulty." Several guards quickly adjusted the bandages around his eyes, strapped his legs and arms to the chair, attached the electrodes to his right leg, and then placed the helmet on his head. Briley sat there for nearly five minutes before the execution was carried out. The corrections director was in touch by telephone with the governor. Shortly before 11 P.M. Governor Charles S. Robb issued the command to "proceed with the order of the court" to execute Briley. The director gave the signal to the prison warden to activate the control panel. Members of the execution team then pushed the button and two fifty-five-second bursts of 2,300 volts of electricity surged through Linwood Briley's body. Richmond Mayor Roy A. West described the scene:

"Walkin' to the 'Lectric Chair"

I Don't want my life to end at Eleven..... But if it does, I Know we will all COME TOGATHER in HEAVEN

I prefer this to be my own way of dying — OTHER than by Force, yet Someone is confused about lifes value, Therefore I say now on this day that one day — Tomorrow — U-HE, HE "GOD"

STill Lives On

Linwood E. Briley

Letter written by Linwood Briley just before his execution.

He pressed against the straps, his hands stretched, and then clenched his fists, and then he relaxed. And we waited a few seconds, a minute or so, and then another surge hit him. . . and when the second one hit him, muscular reaction caused him to surge again against the straps.

TD, October 13, 1984, p. 1

Linwood Briley was pronounced dead at 11:05 P.M.

It was a merciful death, some of the witnesses asserted, much less brutal than what Linwood's victims had suffered. Others were appalled as they saw "his knees burst open—just like fire, you could see the smoke coming from them" as the powerful electric current surged through his body (comments of one observer, interview, Richmond, summer, 1985).[20] Mayor West, after observing this execution and the later execution of James Briley, reportedly declared, "I saw the ultimate examples of justice comparable to the ultimate horror of their crimes. I have no desire to see any more executions" (TD, August 10, 1985, p. B-1).

Since early evening, crowds estimated at between three and five hundred had been gathering outside the penitentiary, some to protest and others to support the execution.

At some churches in the area prayer vigils were held to protest the execution. Several people marched from the churches to the prison, carrying candles and signs reading, "No State Murder" and "Choose Life." They joined others protesting the death penalty outside the penitentiary on Spring Street in praying and singing. They sang "Amazing Grace," and "Cumbayah," and "We Shall Overcome." Among them was the daughter of one of Briley's victims (Richmond Afro-American, October 20, 1984, p. 1).

This was the first time a Black person had been executed in Virginia in twenty-two years,[21] and it was obvious that some bloodthirsty racists of the type for whom lynchings had been festive occasions were determined to make the most of this event. One man carried a hangman's noose on a stick; another carried a sign that said, "Have Mercy on Linwood—Reduce Voltage to 110"; others, men and women, sported signs saying, "Fry Em," "Burn Briley Burn," and "Kill the Negro." Some waved Confed-

"Walkin' to the 'Lectric Chair"

erate flags as they chanted, "Burn, baby, burn," and "Burn, Briley, burn," and "May he burn in hell." Others gleefully chanted, "F-R-Y," screamed, "Fry 'im," and uttered all manner of racial epithets. Two young men wore shower caps, one made of aluminum foil, obviously parodying James Briley's capture wearing a shower cap. Several taunted and hooted at the group protesting the death penalty who were gathered on the other side of the street next to the penitentiary. One yelled, "Those against the death penalty hold Linwood's hand when they throw the switch" (*NL*, October 13, 1984, p. 5). The two groups were kept separated by the police to protect those protesting the execution from those supporting it, who were unanimously described by all as the rowdy group (though not all among them were rowdy); one capital punishment foe called the situation at the penitentiary extremely dangerous and another said it was one of the ugliest crowd scenes she had ever witnessed and suggested that the two groups be further separated during any later executions. As the hour for the execution drew near, the supporters began cheering and then commenced a "jubilant countdown" (*Commonwealth Times*, October 16–23, 1984, p. 1).

When Linwood Briley's death was announced, gasps and sobs could be heard from those protesting his execution; some of those supporting the execution cheered and set off fire crackers. As Briley's lawyers left the penitentiary, police had to protect them from the menacing crowd who yelled and shouted at them. At least fifty policemen had been required to keep order at the scene. Not all of the supporters were crass and obscene in their demonstrations and some were appalled at the racism expressed by their cohorts.

The prisoners in the State Penitentiary could see and hear the crowds outside, but they had to rely on the television for news of the execution itself. They were angry and frustrated as they witnessed the "lynch-mob" scene and heard the crowd yelling racial epithets. One vehemently declared, "If I had been out I'd have been out with a gang on that group out there with their nooses and their signs and yelling 'Kill the nigger' " (conversation, State Penitentiary, November 26, 1984). At eleven o'clock some of the prisoners expressed their protest by cursing, beating on walls, banging their cell doors, and shouting at the officers. One of the prisoners who had been in C-Cell (the solitary confinement building) at the time told me that all was quiet there, however, since those inmates, who had already been under lockdown since September 24 as a security precaution, feared that they would be further punished if they expressed any protest. Several prisoners watched the TV reports of the unfolding events. It was an odd feeling to see some of the scenes outside the prison which they were witnessing being covered live on the TV screen. Then the telecaster announced Linwood's death. The noise and shouting increased. When they later looked out and saw the body being brought up the steps from the basement of A Building and carried to the waiting ambulance, many shouted, "You're a murderer!" "Two wrongs don't make a right!" and similar expressions. Their display received no response from the guards. As one prisoner told me, "They knew we'd get tired sooner or later—and we couldn't do anything" (November 26, 1984).

The next day the Virginia State Penitentiary hosted a social affair/dance. Several of the inmates with whom I talked were convinced that it was designed to pacify the population. Many felt it inappropriate to have a band and dancing and general celebration right after an execution—"dudes acting like ain't nothing happened" (November 26, 1984). They noted that they were served fried chicken the next day and fried fish at the party—and they were allowed to have as much as they wanted. Whenever there is fear of an uprising or some dissension, the men receive better food to pacify them (November 26, 1984).

On October 15, the *News Leader* editorial applauded the execution and justified it, listed the names of the victims of the Briley brothers, and concluded, "Linwood Briley will kill no more" (p. 10).

Linwood Briley was eulogized by Reverend Odie Brown in a private ceremony at a Richmond funeral home.

On March 19, 1985, James Briley was brought to the Virginia State Penitentiary in preparation for his execution, scheduled for April 18, 1985.

"Walkin' to the 'Lectric Chair"

This is a god damn place filled with sorrow
A place where writs, appeals is the only tomorrow
A place where lawyers' messages are left untold
A place where peoples' hearts are filled with hate and
cold

"A Psalm for Death Row," by Larry Batten
Mecklenburg Correctional Center, 1985

According to James Briley, he was abused and taunted after his brother's death: "I was pushed or caught up in corridors and [they were] saying, you know, 'You won't last long; you know what you got in store for you now.' My cell was destroyed many times; they used the rumor of the possibility of another escape [to justify the searches]" (press conference, April 16, 1985).

The ensuing events were basically a replay of his brother's last days. James too remained optimistic. Two days before his execution he called a press conference, in which he, like his brother, acclaimed his innocence and hoped for a miracle: "Each day that I live, I live with hope and I live with faith, and as long as I am alive, that's the way it's going to be" (press conference, April 16, 1985).

As is usual in these cases, appeals and requests for stays were heard until the last minute. On April 18 a stay of execution was requested on the basis of a witness who had come forward to attest to the fact that Duncan Meekins had confessed to her that he was guilty of the murders that Briley was convicted of. That and another appeal were turned down.

Fellow inmates at the State Penitentiary were more dramatic in their protest of James Briley's execution than they had been of his brother's. At about 7:45 A.M. on the morning of the execution inmates from B Building jumped four guards in an attempt to take them hostage in order to stop the execution. Several guards rushed to assist their fellows, and other prisoners joined the fray. The guards were armed with night sticks and the prisoners with a variety of sharp instruments. The melee lasted about twenty minutes, and within an hour, with the help of additonal guards who had been called in in anticipation of this uprising, the prison was under control and the inmates were all under lockdown. Six

Long Gone

guards were hospitalized and three others were treated for minor 139
injuries. One prisoner suffered superficial wounds. James Briley
called home to let his family know that he was not hurt and that
he was sorry about the incident. Later Mrs. Briley, his new wife,
expressed thanks to the inmates for an act which indicated "you
care about James" (*New York Post*, April 19, 1985, p. 24).

That afternoon James Briley spent about two hours with his
mother, his eleven-year-old daughter, his two great aunts, and his
wife. He also spent some of the day listening to music, including
recordings by Al Green. Around 7 P.M. he ate a last meal of
shrimp and drank a soda. Then at 8 o'clock he showered and his
head was shaved. He talked on the telephone with family members; his last words to his wife at 10:36 P.M. were, "Don't worry
about me now—I am free at last" (obituary, April 20, 1985). As
he entered the execution chamber, Briley told the chaplain, "I
love you." He then smiled and twice asked the witnesses, "Are
you happy?" (*New York Post*, April 19, 1985, p. 24). The first charge
of electricity entered his body at 11:02. He was pronounced dead
at 11:07. Moments after the execution, prisoners began breaking
cell windows in protest. They continued breaking windows
throughout the night.

On the morning following the execution, two pictures in the
Times-Dispatch (April 19, 1985, p. E-1) told the story of the repeat
performance at the state penitentiary—one was the picture of the
tear-streaked face of an opponent of the death penalty and the
other the gleeful face of a death proponent. On the night of the
execution, again about two hundred opponents of the death penalty gathered and sang and prayed. About five hundred supporters gathered to hurl racial epithets of the same ilk heard at
his brother's execution and to carry the familiar signs. This time
one demonstrator carried a skeleton with a sign, "This was Linwood." Soon after James's death was announced, someone in the
crowd yelled, "We want Mason!" (Odel Mason, a retarded Black
convict who was executed on June 25 as scheduled; his execution
was a repeat on a smaller scale of the celebration that accompanied the Briley executions. There one white woman carried a
sign reading, "How does it feel to be burned in a chair? Burn—

"Walkin' to the 'Lectric Chair"

damn you—koon!" and shouted, "It's Miller time! We're going to drink after they fry him!" [*TD*, June 26, 1985, p. A-5]).

On April 20, 1985, the editorial in the *News Leader* applauded the fact that "a just society" had enacted its vengeance (p. 12).

James Briley was eulogized by Dr. Darrell Rollins in a private ceremony at the same Richmond funeral home as his brother Linwood. He was buried in North Carolina.

An unintended irony was highlighted in the *Times-Dispatch* on April 14, 1985. One of the headlines (on page D-1) read, "Slayings are on rise. . ." and another on the same page announced, "State execution rate may be rising soon," a juxtaposition which unintentionally pointed out a correlation that many are noting between the execution rate and the murder rate, though there remains debate about which is the cause and which is the effect. Although countless studies have purported to show that there is no indication that capital punishment deters murderers and some suggest that, conversely, murder rates seem to escalate after state executions, the debate goes on. In July 1985 Roy West, the Black mayor of Richmond, provoked a furor when he proclaimed his support for capital punishment as a deterrent to crime.

West's comments were motivated by the release of crime statistics regarding murders committed in the city. Richmond, which witnessed one execution in 1984 and two in 1985, set a near record for homicides (80) in 1984, and an all-time record in 1985 of 94, exceeding by 6 the previous record of 88 murders that occurred in 1972, several of which were related to a drug war. The record murder rate of 1985 slowed between April 14 and May 22. Sgt. Norman Harding speculated that James Briley's execution on April 18 may have served as a deterrent (*TD*, July 7, 1985, p. C-1). But within a month of the execution of Morris Odell Mason on June 25, ten slayings occurred.

As Virginians continued to debate whether executions discourage or stimulate murders and whether murderers should be executed, Virginians are, unfortunately, finding no solutions, but they are achieving dubious distinctions in both areas of this revolving post-hoc dilemma: Virginia, which has executed the youngest convicts (two twelve-year-old slave boys) and which has executed the only brothers since the Furman moratorium, leads the nation in the total number of executions through the years; and Richmond, capital of Virginia and site of its executions, in 1985 (with 94 murders in a city of 218,000) had the second highest homicide rate in the nation, ranking behind only Detroit, according to a projection by the *Times-Dispatch* (February 3, 1985, p. B-1).

"Walkin' to the 'Lectric Chair"

CHAPTER 8

A Legend
in the Making

*Folk Responses
to the Great Escape*

Practically from the moment the Great Escape began, the individuals involved, especially the Brileys, and every episode in the drama of their breakout, their flight, their capture, and their execution provoked responses from a wide variety of the folk. Poems, songs, memorates, jokes, quips, sketches, photocopied materials, bumper stickers, T-shirts, caps—the whole gamut of folk responses—acclaimed their feat, mocked their failures, derided their captors, and in other ways recorded and began to memorialize their escapades in manners that have all the characteristics of a developing legend.

Clearly an initial tendency of some segments of the Black folk community was to view the escapees, especially the Brileys, in the tradition of the Baad Nigger on the run. The Baad Nigger has a long tradition as a favorite character in Black folklore, beginning with the slaves' Brer Rabbit and Slave John and attaining the more contemporary expression in the likes of the Great MacDaddy, Railroad Bill, Dolemite, Shine, and Stagolee. All of these personae are characterized by their absolute rejection of established authority figures—Ole Massa, the sheriff, the judge. In the tales and toasts that recount their exploits, they are acclaimed for acts that are generally regarded as negative: stealing, seducing, whoring, pimping, fighting, gambling, killing. They are, especially in their more recent manifestations, men who are angry and hostile, tough and violent, who shoot up drugs and shoot down people, who court death constantly and don't fear dying, who sport big cars, fine rags, and flashy women, who flaunt their criminal activities in the eyes of the authorities and dare them to attempt to restrain them. These heroes often end up in jail or in hell, but like Brer Rabbit in the briar patch, this is their element, and they operate in jail or hell as they did on the streets and in the bars and pool halls —the "jungles" that make up their world.

Many observers have been nonplussed at the popularity of such a negative figure, one who has almost no redeeming characteristics—he is not fighting his white opponents to change conditions in society, but to achieve some selfish personal end; he is just as likely to cold-bloodedly shoot down a drinking buddy or his woman as "to off" the policeman. He is not governed by any morals, laws, or rules. He owes no allegiance to any person or nation. He has no conscience. Why then his continuing appeal?

Probably the most attractive feature of this character is precisely his rejection of the authority, laws, and values of a system that does not value Blacks and his assertion of his own power and authority, something that many who cheer him can only vicariously enjoy. Furthermore, psychiatrists William H. Grier and Price M. Cobbs suggest that Blacks empathize with his fear and anger and hostility because they must daily repress those same emotions to achieve respectability: "every black man harbors a potential bad nigger inside him," they maintain.[1] Through their pleasure in his outrageous actions in these tales they can release their own pent up emotions. As Roger Abrahams puts it in his discussion of the broader group of trickster heroes who indulge in anti-social activity, "His celebrated deeds function as an approved steam-valve for the group."[2]

In addition to Blacks who find him attractive as a figure through whose escapades they can vicariously express the hostility and aggressiveness that they must in reality repress, it is important to note a growing subculture, especially among teenage gangs, some adolescent groups, drug cultures, and certain other sectors within Black ghettos and prisons, who in reality adopt their own system of values, style of life, and rules of behavior, which are often diametrically opposed to the values of the larger society. To them such a character is not an escapist fantasy; he is a model for emulation. Such a response, as unfortunate and terrifying as it may be, is not merely understandable; it is inevitable. As even Thomas Jefferson noted in his *Notes on the State of Virginia*, "The man, in whose favour no laws of property exist, probably feels himself less bound to respect those made in favour of others" (p. 142).

Consequently, at least within some segments of the Black community, the response to the tendency of the larger society to ignore or justify and condone violence toward the Black man at the same time it prohibits and violently punishes violence perpetrated by him (especially if it is directed against whites) has been to "change the joke and slip the yoke," to acclaim the rebellion of Blacks against that same society and to attack and destroy all that it holds dear, including its work ethics, its political principles, its moral values.

Clearly among the features that make the Baad Nigger so popular are his attainment of items expressive of great wealth—cars, clothes, jewels, beautiful women—and many of those who relish these tales can envision attaining such wealth only through illegal means. That they choose to esteem such ephemeral expressions of wealth rather than property and homes and businesses reflects how limited are their aspirations, even in fantasy.

Finally what makes the Baad Nigger so attractive is his style—something that is immediately highlighted in most of the toasts treating him. As Charles A. Frye notes, "For blacks. . . style has always been important—so much so that the word has become a verb. And the Badman, he be Stylin' for days. He is obsessed with it. . . . In fact, black machismo can probably be best described as a style-suffused mode of behavior. . . . The very essence of the Badman is style—it is evident in the way they wear their clothes—from the hat to the shoes, the way they walk, the way they interact with their women—but more importantly the way they interact with other black men."[3]

Folk reactions to the escape that tend to relate it to the traditional Baad Nigger focus almost exclusively on the Brileys. Good

A Legend in the Making

looking, impressive, commanding, stylish, intimidating, popular, the Brileys seemed with their constant supply of money,
drugs, and women to be the mold out of which the Baad Nigger
was created. Then when they masterminded a plot that resulted
in the biggest escape ever accomplished from a Death Row in this
country—AND pulled it off with such *style*, bards began to record
their exploits, placing them in the company of other famed outlaws and Baad niggers:

Sitting in a cage, waiting up on Death Row
Where limited is your age
And from here your life must go.
And *go* they *did*.
But first the judge said, "From here you must go,
You know you ain't see no bridge
Where the poor don't pay the toll."
But like Jesse and Frank James of old
(or so the story has been told),
Two BA'AD motherfuckers and four others
Escaped from Mecklenburg, Virginia's Death Row.

The t.v. screamed out the announcer's shout,
"You better get in doors and lock your house!
Shut out the lights, get your weapons out,
Some *fool* motherfuckers are loose, running about!"
It hit all the networks on the American scene,
It hit South America, North Greenland, and even Argentine,
That the prison security model for the *whole* wide world
Was *bust* wide open,
Split at the damn seams.

But yet I wonder if they did the crimes
Because most bad niggers would have left
    bodies (hundreds!) in a *line*!
But yet they escaped but without any *hate*.
Now they are caught;
Back their bodies have been brought.
Now the death chair's fire will shine.
It has been said by many signifying niggers
That the move was a class act, a work of art.

Long Gone

As always, there's the other hand,
Saying they *should* have blowed the system apart!

But as the switch is set and all the circuits are set,
I wonder if they're guilty of the charges they've met.
And if so, they're only reflecting society's flow—
A hundred and eighteen thousand in Hiroshima,
A land once inhabited by Indians,
Gunsmoke, rifleman, viciousness is the way they go.

Charles Satchell, Virginia State
Penitentiary, August 6, 1984

When the Brileys escaped,
they did it with style and simple grace.

Now the man called them killers on a tear,
But we knew the brothers was only escaping from despair.

People said they saw them everywhere—down South,
    in woods, in the hills,
Hell, the brothers was up in Philly drinking and
    eating ribs.

I was there the night the man was fooled
And the brothers took flight.
The man told everyone they had a bomb,
But if he told it right, you know he fell for an old
    move, a dance and a song.

Now if you are at the bar buying drinks
Get a bottle of the best grapes
And lift your glass to the brothers and
the night of the Great Escape.

Harry Seigler, Mecklenburg
Correctional Center, March 1985

Late one night in the heat of May
Six brave comrades made their getaway.
No doubt they had a *master* plan
They used their minds to escape from the man.
Out came the guards with their sniffing dogs
Sniffing the scent that led over hollow logs
Two were caught not far away
Their freedom lasted only half a day.

A Legend in the Making

Two more were captured after a long, hard chase.
Two more back in the joint! Oh, what a waste!
Now all six have been captured again,
But the odds seemed against them from beginning to end.

Joseph Jones, Virginia State
Penitentiary, August 6, 1984

The Brileys. . . played some hell of a part [in the planning
and execution of the escape]. I also give them credit for going
out in *style*.

Red, Virginia State Penitentiary,
April 29, 1985

The following conversation among inmates at Mecklenburg Correctional Center reflects some of the men's reactions to the escape, their delight in the exploits of the convicts and in the humiliation of the guards. Their offtimes blasphemous and irreverant account contains the kinds of exaggerations and embellishments that such accounts tend to assume with the passing of time:

"Colonel————let me out to make a phone call. . . . When I got through my phone call, he let me go around the corner. Two hours later I seen that nigger—ain't have NO clothes man, I seen 'im."

"————went inside and took his shoes off and start playin' spades. One guy went and hid in the bathroom. Linwood told ————to get that book, right. ————opened the door and came out and soon as he did the nigger came right out of the bathroom on his ass. Linwood came down the hall like this, eased down the hall like this, stood just like this [I am unable to describe action, but tone suggests pleasure in the dramatization and acclamation of Linwood's moves]."

"What really got me was when that Nigger TRICK that bitch downstairs. TRICKED that whore! Lock that bitch in the closet downstairs all by herself. He got Hawkins to call downstairs and say that a officer was coming to release her. Peterson went right downstairs on the elevator, walked right over to the bitch, told her to open the door—SCHUTT, SCHUTT, SCHUTT [sounds, indicating getting something done]————locked her ass right

Long Gone

across the———SCHUTT, SCHUTT, SCHUTT! Start working the [control room] door."

"Easy, easy, easy as a motherfucker."

"Hell, they coulda let everybody out. That ain't no lie. They coulda took over this whole goddamn institution. The WHOLE institution! Anytime this nigger can go over to Building 5 and BACK, and these sonavabitches still don't know what's going ON. Then they call a van in and a officer come in and still don't know who they IS!"

"The reason they didn't do that was because they didn't have that in their plans. They just wanted to get out. They didn't want to take over the institution. They just wanted to get the fuck out."

"I seen that fat dude, Tuggle, I seen him runnin', but when I seen 'im he had his face shaved, and I thought he was a officer, right? Then Red came 'round the corner with pō-lice clothes on, right, and did like that. Man them niggers had machetes like that, made out o' that motherfuckin' tin shit. That shit'll cut [unclear]. Yes suh! That shit'll cut on a machine. . . . The red dude—he still over there, right? He left out of the building and went to Building 5. When you get to Building 5 at night, it's dark, right there by the gate, right, and he stood right there by the gate, right. And he stood right there, and that officer that got fired, he went to the Administration Building and got a pair of motherfuckin' fire [extinguishers]. I sat right there and watched 'im. But it wasn't none of my business. Me and [he lists six others], and damn, I forget the other nigger's name—sat right there and watched 'em. Watched 'em go out the door. The only part we couldn't see, when they went out the sally port gates. That's the only part we couldn't see."

"They was gon' kill 'em all, right?"

"But Turner stopped that."

"Yeah. Tell me they was gon' kill all the guards. You damn right."

June 1985
(in a few instances the order of this conversation
has been changed for coherence)

Prisoners with whom I talked were almost unanimous in applauding the escape as a class act pulled off by some Baad dudes.

A Legend in the Making

While a few complained about the restrictions that they had to suffer as a result, most focused their antagonism for that discomfort against the authorities rather than the Brileys. Almost all agreed that imprisoned men, especially condemned men, would naturally seek freedom. Only one prisoner, a Death Row inmate, assailed the escape as a futile effort that ultimately caused additional suffering to everybody, including the escapees (Mecklenburg, February 28, 1985).

Most prisoners, however tended to express disappointment in their capture. Here the Brileys disillusioned those who saw them in the role of the Baad Nigger whom they admired. Prisoners expected and hoped that they would not have returned without a fight, and some condemned them for their unresisting surrender: "I can't understand why they allowed themselves to be captured—they should have shot it out. The only hero is a dead hero" (inmate, Virginia State Penitentiary, November 26, 1984); another man told me that there had been a rumor that Linwood had been killed in a shootout with police in Tidewater, and several inmates agreed that it would have been better to have died defending his freedom; one proceeded to insist, "None of us here should die in the pen of a heart attack or any natural cause. If we die in here, we should be killed fighting for our freedom and our dignity" (ibid.) A Mecklenburg inmate insisted, "They wouldn't got me alive. That's for damn sure. That's one thing—and I know I'm gon' burn!" "No way," another assented (June 1985).

The capture of all of the escapees was frequently lampooned in conversations, poems, and the like. Typical are these comments from a rap session at Mecklenburg:

> "When they escaped, they did the dumbest things. I don't know why they went to Philadelphia."
> "They say Lem Tuggle did a lot of snitching. But, hey, man, that nigger was moving along—way up there near Vancouver area."
> "And stopped in a gift store and robbed it!"
> "With a motherfuckin' machete!"
> "And now he up on *Death Row*! Shoulda built him a log cabin up in the mountains there somewhere and stayed!"

Long Gone

"I'd a went and hunt me some wild animals, man!"

"I think the escape came off decent. But after they got out that's when they got ignorant."

"What about them other two dumb dudes sittin' in the laundromat drinking wine and eating cheese!"

[general laughter]

"That's ridiculous!"

"Damn sure is. Down in NORTH CAROLINA. Ku Klux Klan country! They lucky they didn't kill 'em up there."

"Damn sure is. They lucky they didn't send them on the State Farm and kill 'em. They got some RED necks on the State Farm."

Mecklenburg, June 1985

The few indications I have of the responses of white inmates suggest that they tended to associated with Tuggle. One inmate wrote to me, summarizing their comments: "All the newspapers were concern about was the blacks, as if the white man wasn't even a death row escapee. Tuggle was the only one with enough sense to at least really try to get away. The dudes (Brileys) got out, but they were some dumb dudes, laying back eating chicken and living with known relatives" (letter from Mecklenburg inmate, March 1985).

While inmates tend to applaud the escape and satirize the officials in their folklore, folk items which I have been able to find circulating among agents of the law tend to lampoon the blunders of the escapees, to play on some stereotypes, and to focus on their capture. Some of those pieces may give some lip service to the image of the Bad Man, but they are more likely to deflate it. They are also more likely to jest about the execution. A mimeographed "letter" mimics James Briley's capture in a shower cap with his hands over his eyes and mocks his execution. Attached to the original "letter" was an actual shower cap still in its plastic bag; on it was written "Official James Briley Shower Cap / A Mecklenburg Production." I could not determine whether the letter which I saw on the bulletin board of an FBI office in June originated before or after the execution.

Numerous other law officials told me that James's capture in a shower cap was a subject of jokes among their colleagues, but

A Legend in the Making

Congratulations!

You are one of a very few carefully selected individuals chosen to receive one of the first

OFFICIAL JAMES BRILEY SHOWER CAPS

(One size fits all)

Wear it with pride as James did. Useful for formal occasions, costume parties or everyday wear. Terrific for disguises or Halloween outings (Hold hands over eyes & say "Trick or Treat")

Instructions

May be worn centered upon head or tilted to left, right or rear. (Do not tilt toward front except when sleeping.)

Caution

Although this product will protect the wearer from low voltages it will afford no protection from extremely high voltages such as those occurring in lightning bolts and electrical chairs.

This is the story of James and Linwood
They killed everybody in their neighborhood
So they sent them down to Mecklenburg
And the rest is history if you haven't heard.
What they did, they say couldn't be done
But the plan they had made it look like fun.

Notice and poem found on the bulletin board of an FBI office. Grateful acknowledgment is made to Kimberly Pugh for the sketch of James Briley, which replaces the UPI photograph that appeared on the original flyer.

Long Gone

They tricked some guards into falling for their caper;
Told the pretty young nurse they'd be back to rape her later.
The six of them jumped into a van,
Said goodbye to Pod B, See ya later man!
Drove right through the gates headed down to N.C.
How's that for maximum security?
Away they drove down to Warrenton,
their first day of freedom had just begun.
But it didn't last long for Derrick and Earl,
the dumbest murderers in the world.
Instead of making an attempt to flee,
they stuck around to do their laundry.
They were quite surprized as they sipped on their wine
To hear a State Trooper say "Its back to Mecklenburg time."
The other four were making their way
Up the East Coast to Philadelphia, PA.
It was there that Lem and Willie said Goodbye
to the Briley boys, and to Vermont they did fly.
Where the air is cool and the syrup sweet,
they camped out in a tent as their retreat.
But as time wore on and they didn't have a dime,
Lem was forced to commit a crime.
He stole some cash and made his getaway,
but his freedom wouldn't last another day.
Not far from there a call went out in earnest
from Willie Leroy to Mommie Dearest
"Willie, please come home", she said with a cry,
"turn yourself in before you die."
All that was left was the Briley brothers,
but everybody knew they were badder than the others.
The question was Where could they be?
Carolina, Quebec or old Virginny?
When all the time they were doing ducky
Working in a garage as Slim and Lucky.
They did a lotta drugs and had a lotta women.
Philadelphia Freedom - they were really livin'.
Their whereabouts was a mystery
Thanks to the assistance of Uncle Johnny.
Til that fateful night of the barbeque,
grilling chicken on the street and sippin a brew.
Slim was about to chomp down on a thigh
When he saw fifty agents from the FBI.
It happened so quick there was no time to race,
"Put your leg in my hand and wipe that smile off your face."
That ain't no way to treat a felon,
"I didn't get to finish my watermelon.
I'm innocent, I won't take this rap
and I don't want you messin with my shower cap."
Now they're back in Richmond at the Va. State Pen,
they're locked up tight so they won't break out again.
Now there's nothing left; they won't be going nowhere,
Cuz they're both gonna fry in the electric chair!
If after this poem you need a closer look,
you'll just have to wait for the movie or the book....

A Legend in the Making

nobody recounted a specific one. Another item on that same bulletin board was an anonymous poem treating the escape and the capture.

The bulletin board of one office that I visited at the Virginia State Penitentiary had no materials directly related to the Great Escape, but it displayed several cartoons and photocopied sheets spoofing the ACLU, escapes from prison, and employment within the correctional system, all of which subjects received increased attention as a result of the escape. On the end table of the office was a small tree with a hangman's noose on it.

Some of the few items that I was able to collect from guards at Mecklenburg focused on their fear of homosexual rape during the takeover. According to one anecdote, one of the guards who had been forced to disrobe was threatened by a prisoner with a long shank. The guard told the inmate, "You can kill me with that shank if you want to, but just don't get behind me" (Mecklenburg, February 28, 1985). Another anecdote notes that while most of the hostages were in one area when they were rescued, one was found locked in a closet. "Everybody always asks him what he was *doing* in that closet!" (ibid.)

One inmate at the Virginia State Penitentiary who had previously been at Mecklenburg related to me a couple of quips presumably from the escapees during the escape. According to my source, some guys said when the escaping men passed by them dressed in guards' uniforms, as a joke they yelled, "Hey, man, give me some toilet tissue," and the escapees laughed and said, "I ain't no pig" (guard). One inmate who had on a sergeant's uniform reportedly bragged, "Well, at least I've been a sergeant before" (Virginia State Penitentiary, November 26, 1984).

In their personal anecdotes about the escape several of the escapees have made a point of the fact that they did not *break* out. Linwood Briley told Reverend Odie Brown, "We didn't *break* out, we walked out" (telephone conversation with Reverend Brown, June 13, 1985). Most of the escapees have numerous humorous and suspenseful tales about the takeover of the prison, the search for a car in North Carolina, experiences on the road to Philadelphia and Vermont, and the captures. Some of these, such as the account of the fleeing felons stopping to help stranded motorists on the highway, have been frequently recounted, and, containing as they do elements that appeal to the folk imagination, may become a permanent item in accounts of the flight.

Virginia's high level government officials were frequently the butt of jokes about the escapes. Typical was Phil Bagley's observation that Governor Robb had brought many changes to Virginia: "He changed the bumper sticker that used to read, 'Virginia is for lovers.' It now reads, 'When it comes to prisons, Virginia is for leavers' " (*TD*, February 24, 1985, p. C-1). Often the officials deflected some of the attacks upon them through their own self-deflating jests. As he toured the yet unopened new Nottoway Correctional Center, Corrections Director Landon, for example, quipped, "I'm especially proud of this institution because it's the only one we have where we haven't had an escape" (*TD*, July 12, 1984, p. A-7).

One Virginia State Senate hopeful, soundly defeated in the last elections, was motivated by the escape to devise a new kind of lottery while attempting to raise money for his campaign for the 1987 election. He offered a $5,000 reward to the person who came closest to predicting the date and hour of the execution of the six escapees. People sending entries were encouraged to include "a political contribution of at least $5" (*TD*, July 15, 1984, p. F-2).

Radio announcers and newspaper cartoonists were never at a loss for comical responses to the unfolding drama of the escape. The most popular was probably the Brookins cartoon of June 3, 1984, which appeared in the *Times-Dispatch*. The cartoon has been widely reproduced, frequently appearing on T-shirts. Brookins shows a building labeled "Mecklenburg Maximum Security Correctional Center" being carted off by six pairs of legs in striped convict uniforms, while the guards look on with expressions ranging from perplexity to complacency.

One Brookins cartoon—"The Sightings Continue"— in the *Times-Dispatch* shows five groups of people in widely scattered

A Legend in the Making

"I TOLD YOU THAT SHOWER CAP WAS A LOUSY DISGUISE!!"

Grateful acknowledgment is made to Richmond Newspapers, Inc., for permission to use the above cartoons by Gary Brookins. The cartoons appeared in the *Times-Dispatch* on June 3, 1984 (top) and June 21, 1984 (bottom).

Long Gone

Grateful acknowledgment is made to Richmond Newspapers, Inc., for permission to use the above cartoons by Bob Gorrell. The cartoons appeared in the *News Leader* on June 20, 1984 (top) and June 22, 1984 (bottom).

A Legend in the Making

Cartoon by B. Curtis, from *Fysk Magazine*, Summer 1984.

Long Gone

communities of the world who are fearful that the Brileys are
nearby. Another popular Brookins cartoon that appeared in the
Times-Dispatch on June 21, 1984, mimics the shower cap.

The June 20 Gorrell cartoon shows a monoply card, inscribed
"Bearer is Entitled to Get Out of Jail Free," with the notation that
it was confiscated from the Brileys. Gorrell's June 22 cartoon
shows a subdued Linwood Briley thinking that he would rather
be in Philadelphia as he is being led to his Death Row cell. A
cartoon by B. Curtis is *Fysk Magazine* (Summer 1984) commented
on prison life and executions.

Within a month of the escape "The Ballad of the Briley Brothers," a hilarious song composed by two Lynchburg radio station
employees, Randy Graham and Matt McCall, was being heard on
the air. The song recounted the ease with which the Brileys and
their four companions "checked out" of Mecklenburg, tipping
their hats as they drove away, and were "on the road again" in
their borrowed suits. The song mocked the efforts of the law
officials to capture the Brileys, asserting that the local police and
the FBI were getting angry at the Brileys because "you're never
where you're supposed to be."

Throughout the events surrounding the escape, radio announcers and disc jockeys poked fun at the escapees and the authorities. One broadcaster announced a travel ad for a "Mecklenburg
Great Escape Weekend," offering tickets to Vermont, North Carolina, and Canada for the price of a fire extinguisher. When Lem
Tuggle was captured, one station purported to run "advertise-
ments" by Tuggle's hairdresser: "Can you imagine having the
curly locks of Lem Tuggle? Wouldn't you like to be seen bare-
chested with a vest?"

Other jokes were heard around the community. Reportedly a
travel agency advertised its latest tour: "Serve time in a Virginia
prison and see the world." According to one letter to the editor
of the *News Leader*, an announcement was made at a local bowling
alley on the night of the execution of Linwood Briley: "There's a
telephone call for Linwood Briley . . . it's the Governor" (*NL*,
October 19, 1984, p. 14).

Numerous material items have sprung up in response to the

A Legend in the Making

Great Escape. In Richmond, one man made a deck of Briley Brothers Cards spoofing the escapees. In Boydton, hats were sold sporting the logo, "Boydton, VA—site of the famous escape." In several areas T-shirts were available with "The Great Escape" and the Brookins cartoon on them. In Warrenton, North Carolina, someone reported seeing T-shirts with "I am NOT one of the Briley Brothers" written on them.

Obviously the Great Escape is too recent an event for it to be possible to even begin to judge its ultimate impact on folklore. The widespread reactions to the event as it unfolded may remain only the individual responses of some observers, and while such personal responses to a sensational event are clearly of interest and significance to the folklorist, only time will tell whether any of these will be adopted and passed on by the folk so that they may indeed become a part of traditional folklore. I would speculate (a dangerous endeavor, admittedly) that most of the materials arising in the white community are topical in terms of their focus on a specific event occurring at the time (quips about the capture of a particular inmate, the execution of another and the like); thus deriving their effectiveness from an awareness of current events, they will soon be forgotten—the quip about Tuggle's curly hair and his vest is funny only to those who recall his pictures in the paper upon his capture; the Great Escape T-shirts will soon lose their appeal. Other items from the white community such as "The Ballad of the Briley Brothers" and the poem "This is the story of James and Linwood" are catchy parodies of the Black toast that may prove to have a wider and a more lasting appeal, particularly if they are promoted—there are plans to release a record of "The Ballad."

Several of the poems written by individual Black poets about the escape are characteristic of the popular Black toast, and I've been told that recently some bards have been working on raps about the event.[4] Although the escape remains at this point an event celebrated in rhymes and songs and personal narratives, largely individual creations not often being passed along in variant forms; and although they have appeared only within this region (Virginia and to a lesser degree, North Carolina) so far as

Daryl Cumber Dance
in a Great Escape T-shirt.
Grateful acknowledgment is
made to Dr. Maurice Duke
for taking the photograph
for this book.

I have been able to determine, it is not too far-fetched, if one
judges the widespread reactions to this event, to speculate that
the exploits of the Brileys may one day enter the Black folk tradition, like those of other Black outlaw heroes such as Stagolee
and Railroad Bill (the legends of whom grew out of actual incidents), as well as those of real-life white outlaw heroes, such as
Jesse James. How their exploits will ultimately be colored and
exaggerated and embellished, one cannot say, though some indications are already apparent in accounts cited throughout this
book. That the setting might be changed to a better known, more

A Legend in the Making

notorious prison seems quite possible; surely Sing-Sing and Alcatraz and Leavenworth, and Folsom, though they might not all be more easily facilitated within the rhyme and rhythm of the verses, might be preferred because they would be more familiar to the audience (the matter of reconciling time and place is not a critical issue—note how easily bards switched the sinking of the Titanic from April to May in most versions of that most famous of all toasts, "The Sinking of the Titanic" or "Shine," probably because of the greater ease of finding rhymes for *May*). Even the names of the principals might be changed (Railroad Bill was actually Morris Slater), though the alliterative "Briley brothers" has the catchy ring required in such accounts—Slim and Lucky, though, have already appeared in parts of at least one account. I cannot here present "The Legend of the Briley Brothers," but given the sensationalism of the crimes attributed to them and the spectacular escape they accomplished, the intensity of the reactions and responses they have provoked, and the mesmeric hold they have taken on the public imagination, I have no doubt that I have been witnessing and recording the initial stages of a legend in the making.

Afterword

Upon beginning this project, I, who had gone through forty-some odd years of life regarded by all who knew me as above reproach and beyond suspicion, suddenly became an object of suspicion and the victim of accusations from *everyone*. Several prisoners were certain that I had been sent in by frustrated authorities to unearth sensitive details that they had not been able to coerce in other ways about the escape and about the individuals involved. Other prisoners thought my forthright and candid questions and direct probe for information revealed a preposterous naivete, if not indeed extreme folly bordering on madness. Authorities were suspicious that I wanted to reveal information that would be embarrassing to them. The convicted men suspected that I proposed to write more of the sensationalized drivel that made them appear dehumanized brutes and ingoramuses. The authorities suspected I intended to romanticize the escapees and their breakout. Upstanding citizens simply didn't know what to think about someone who wanted to talk to men who had killed and raped and committed all manner of crimes. At least one person accused that my pursuit of the project revealed an insensitivity to the plight of the condemned men. Some people expected that I was trying to get them in trouble—it was dangerous to talk about the Brileys (they might strike back at you); it was dangerous for the Brileys to talk (it might hurt their case); it was dangerous to talk about your role in the escape (the authorities might punish you); it was dangerous to reveal what went on in prison (whether an employee or a prisoner, there were all kinds of possible retaliations you might suffer). Some impatiently reprimanded me for providing malefactors a forum they didn't deserve and giving credibility to a criminal act through treating it as a serious subject for study; the pursuit of such an endeavor, they implied, indicated that I had no respect for life or law. Some had never heard of the theme of escape in Black folklore and considered the whole idea a bunch of nonsense. A few people patiently and calmly tried to explain to me reasons that I should seek more appropriate and acceptable projects. Others impatiently and vociferously tried to frighten me out of continuing my project by veiled threats and crude verbal attacks. A few simply attempted through their authority and their positions to malign, restrict, or sabotage my efforts.

But despite their initial suspicion and reluctance, *most* of the people I approached were—sometimes after long discussions and debates—willing and often eager to assist me. Indeed a few of them devoted themselves to helping me to overcome or circumvent some of the problems I was facing and to recommend me to their colleagues and friends. They encouraged me to continue, advised me on how to proceed, warned me of the detractors, and so on. A few of them became so fervently committed to the effective completion of the project that they sometimes expressed impatience and frustration with me because I refused to create the diversions and ploys, tell the lies, pay the money, or make the necessary compromises that would have achieved certain ends for me. Others found it incredulous that I didn't try to expose some of the individuals who thwarted my efforts—especially when those supporters were willing to provide me ammunition, or that I expressed an understanding of and even sympathy for the motivation of some of my detractors. Some reprimanded me for not being a fighter when I didn't try to go over heads to overcome impediments created by certain officials. One prisoner even had his lawyer call to offer assistance when it was clear that officials were taking unusual steps to prevent him from talking to me.

Generally my unwillingness to fight was motivated at least partly through an understanding of the precarious situations of some people involved and perhaps mainly through a belief that discretion is indeed the better part of valor, or—perhaps—as one

Long Gone

prisoner paraphrased it, "You scared." I recognized the hopeless-
ness of involving myself in long fights with officials who, if I
embarrassed them on one front, would create obstacles on others
and might even make life uncomfortable, to put it in its mildest
terms, for some of the inmates who had helped me. One battle
won might mean several more compromised or lost. Furthermore
as a matter of principle, I decided that I had to be absolutely
honest with everyone whom I approached—I would create no
ploys in an effort to gain information and assistance from anyone.
I have no doubt that had such tactics won me some small benefits,
profits, or bits of information, they would ultimately have back-
fired, and the word would have been out on the prison grapevine
and elsewhere in no time.

The project was difficult not only because of the necessity to
solicit the cooperation and to gain the trust of so many individuals, but also because it required walking such a sensitive tight-
rope involving people who feel so adamantly about conflicting
issues, many on one side of the issue not trusting those on the
other, indeed, passionately and vehemently despising them. It
was necessary to try to get to know and to understand the back-
grounds and motivations and personalities of several men who
were convicted of criminal offenses. It was necessary also to
consider their crimes and consequently to recognize the agonies
that their victims and their victims' families had endured. It was
further necessary to comprehend the process by which the agents
of our system of justice had investigated those crimes and prosecuted and punished them. And finally, and most important, it
was necessary to uncover and study and interpret the varied
responses of the folk to this whole situation, some of these responses painfully coarse and brutal. No step in this process was
without its contradictions, though for many involved it was perceived as all black and white. People in such polarized positions
are unlikely to have much sympathy or understanding for one
another, or even to regard with favor someone who is talking to
all of these factions.

The more I explored and discovered and weighed, the more of

Afterword

a challenge it became for me to remain balanced and objective and yet resolute in my presentation. I recognized that some of my "principles" and perceptions had been rather easily established and had never been put to the test. I began this project inexorably opposed to the death penalty. I end this project inexorably opposed to the death penalty, but with less of a tendency to reject so cavalierly and self-righteously the views of those who support it. As I talked with several local detectives, with guards at state penitentiaries and with FBI officials from various areas, I discovered that, obviously influenced by some stereotypes and armed with certain preconceptions, I was surprised at how professional, objective, and committed some of these officials are. Finally as I met and talked with the condemned men and other inmates, I was amazed at how unlike the stereotype of the hardened, vicious criminal many of them seemed. One cannot interact with and get to know many of these men without feeling a great sense of the loss of human potential and without agonizing over whether a society as great as ours does not have the resources to try to emphasize prevention and rehabilitation and not just punishment. One cannot contemplate the reality of life in even our most advanced prisons without being appalled at the recognition that all too often they compound and create problems rather than solve them, that they brutalize and criminalize men rather than rehabilitate them. Obviously this expansion of my awareness does not negate the reality of the racist supporter of the death penalty who yells "Kill the nigger!" Nor does it negate the reality of the brutal policeman who casually abuses young Black men much more commonly than whites (*Essence* recently pointed to reports that show that minorities are nine times more likely than whites to be shot and killed by police, September 1985, p. 92). Nor does it negate the reality of the depraved killer and rapist and robber who, given the opportunity, will offend again. And certainly it does not negate the harsh reality of the suffering and anger and frustrations of the victims of crime. What it does point up most shockingly is how little the balanced, well-meaning, most moderate members of these varied factions whom

Long Gone

fate so cruelly and inextricably casts together recognize and understand about the other. Clearly this book cannot provide many
answers, but I hope it will motivate readers to be more open to
recognizing and attempting to understand the complex dimen-
sions of the problem.

Afterword

Notes

Chapter 1

1. William H. Grier and Price M. Cobbs, *Black Rage* (New York: Bantam Books, 1969), p. 31.

2. This is not to suggest that Blacks have not tried all of these means in their efforts to achieve freedom. From the beginning, individual slaves petitioned in the courts for freedom and other rights, while other slaves organized slave rebellions; and throughout their history in America, Blacks have organized in political, civic, and religious groups that sought redress through the approved channels.

3. Air out, back off, backtrack, beat it, blow, breeze, brush off, bust out, cop a drill/trot, crash out, cruise, cut, cut out, cut and run, depart, disappear, dodge, drift, duck out, ease on out, ease on down, escape, fade, flake out/off, flee, fly, fly the coop, foot it, freewheel, get on in/off/down/out/back, go, go away, go North, go over the hill/wall, grab a armful of box-cars/the first thing smoking, hat up, haul ass/it, hightail it, hike, hit the road/street, hoof it, hustle, journey, jump bail, jump a train, lam (or take a lam), leave, light out, make feet help the body, make it, make oneself scarce, make tracks, ooze, percolate, ride, ride the rails, roll out/on, run, scat, scram, sell out, shove, shove off, skip, skivver, slide, space, split, step, take a powder/duck, take off, take to the woods/hills/road, trilly on, trilly walk, trot, truck, truck it, tunnel (go into hiding), vamoose, wheel it, wing it.

4. In their folklore, Negroes always associate the rabbit with themselves.

5. I do not mean by this discussion to imply that the theme of running, of escape, is unique to Black literature. It may be said to be the common theme in a country founded and populated by a host of peoples running from religious oppression, political oppression, poverty, and imprisonment. The theme laid out in

the diaries and travelogues of the Founding Fathers continues as several of our major White writers, such as Irving, Cooper, Melville, Twain, and Faulkner, recorded the journeys of men fleeing everything from domineering wives to the restrictions of organized society. Given the history of Blacks in this country, the theme does, however, have unique implications and variations within the Black tradition.

6. *The Negro American,* ed. Talcott Parsons and Kenneth B. Clark (Boston: Houghton, 1966), p. 258.

7. It is interesting to observe that the runner, the legendary hero in Black folklore, and the warrior, the legendary hero in the Western tradition, were ironically counterposed in newspaper accounts of the Great Escape, which shared the headlines from the day the escape was announced (June 1, 1984) and the ensuing days with recollections of D-Day.

8. The blues are full of lines of men being "judged without a trial," and folktales treating the theme of injustice in the courtroom are legion. For additional examples, see Ch. 8.

Chapter 2

1. The men in blue are officers; the one in white is the superior officer. The inmate/speaker was being transferred from the State Farm to Mecklenburg, a much dreaded transfer for prisoners in any state prison, especially before the post-escape reforms. In August 1985 a prisoner with whom I have frequently worked in the Creative Writing Program at the Virginia State Penitentiary called me and said, "Guess where I am." The tone of his voice told me all—Mansion in the Back (Mecklenburg).

2. The following information about the Mecklenburg Correctional Center is based upon a variety of sources, including a brochure on the institution prepared by the Department of Corrections of the Commonwealth of Virginia, a report prepared by James D. Henderson of the National Institute of Corrections (June 27, 1984), the "Report of the Mecklenburg Correctional Center Study Committee" (November 7, 1984), personal visits to Mecklenburg, interviews, newspaper accounts in a variety of papers, including the *TD,* the *NL,* and the *Post,* and televised news accounts.

3. For a more detailed description of these categories, see the "Report of the Mecklenburg Study Committee," pp. 16-20, 25-78.

4. The following reconstruction of the plans for the escape and the execution of it is based upon a variety of sources, including,

most notably, the report of Gary L. Bass, then warden of Mecklenburg, to Robert M. Landon, then director of the Department of Corrections, June 5, 1984, and other reports of investigating agencies; interviews with Robert M. Landon; interviews, telephone conversations, and correspondence with numerous inmates who were incarcerated at Mecklenburg at the time of the escape, including six Death Row inmates, televised news accounts, and accounts in several newspapers (especially the *TD*, the *NL*, the *Post*, and the *Pilot*).

I have chosen not to use the actual names of participants who did not flee when their comments might be sensitive or self-incriminating except in instances when those comments were made to news media and were widely disseminated. This has created a situation whereby a couple of the inmates are identified in some sections but are referred to by a pseudonym in others.

5. Red explained to me that during his trial for murder he had decided "if they sentence me to death, I'm gone" (telephone conversation, April 29, 1985). When he did in fact receive the death sentence, he already had things rigged up so that he could open up his Courtland Jail cell (Southampton County) at will: "I had it set up so I could walk in and out whenever I wanted to." Indeed, he insisted, he could open up the other cells too: "I could have opened the whole jail up. I could have taken a whole lot with me on that one." He noted that both in his escape from Courtland and in the planning for the Mecklenburg escape, he insisted upon accomplishing the escape without violence. When he escaped from Courtland on January 6, 1980, it was several hours before the authorities even recognized that he was gone. Red was recaptured on January 7, 1980 (telephone conversation, June 30, 1985). He had previously escaped from Unit #22 (Tidewater Correctional Unit) in Chesapeake City on November 17, 1971. He was recaptured on January 5, 1972. Red seems not to regard that escape as noteworthy since it was simply a matter of walking away from a road camp and did not require the ingenuity needed to execute the other escapes. When I asked about this earlier escape, which he had never mentioned in the three previous conversations we had had (and which I only discovered in checking his records), he responded, "Oh, there was nothing to that— I just walked away from a road camp" (June 30, 1985). Another inmate relayed (with Red's approval) his method in that earlier escape: "Every day he'd play with the guards by saying, "I'm running," and hide behind trees laughing. He'd roll on the ground acting like a dumb fun nigga. They laughed along with

Note to Page 16

him. Then one day he was gone, really running" (letter from a Mecklenburg inmate, June 27, 1985).

6. This revelation caused Acting Warden Sherman Townley to insist that Stockton "will be one of the most difficult inmates to house and keep secure. . . . [he] has signed his death warrant. . . . [his] future is very dim" (*NL*, August 18, 1984, p. 5).

7. This and other references to Stockton's diary are from the *Pilot*, Sept. 16, 1984.

8. The magnitude of this plan is matched by a similar earlier unsuccessful plan for an escape from Death Row in Jamaica's St. Catherine District Prison. There, led by Mario Hector, inmates secured and concealed weapons with which they nightly filed their cell doors, concealing the cuts with a mixture of cooked rice, soap, and the dust from the cuts. Twenty-five of the twenty-six condemned men on that Death Row were to participate in the escape. When their plans were completed, they waited several days until December 26, 1974, when there was only one sentry on duty. Someone called him and asked for a glass of water. When he delivered the water, four prisoners with drawn knives took him hostage. They were unable to get outside the prison, but, holding their hostage, they demanded and got a meeting with Prime Minister Michael Manley that ultimately resulted in extensive prison reforms in Jamaica and in a review of the cases of several of the condemned men and in the commutation of the death sentences of nine of them (see Mario Hector, *Death Row*, London: Zed Books, 1984).

9. Portions of this press conference were broadcast over the three major networks. WXEX-TV, Channel 8, Richmond, allowed me to view and record their entire video tape of the press conference.

10. These assignments are detailed in Stockton's diary in a March 1984 entry.

11. There were twenty-four prisoners, the full capacity, assigned to Death Row at the time; however, one was not there the night of the escape because he was away for a court hearing. Two more prisoners had been sentenced to death in Virginia, but they had not been transferred to Mecklenburg.

12. In his diary Stockton attacks the above accounts of Evans' role and charges that Evans was a part of the planning and the execution of the escape and only later helped the hostages in order to get the heat off himself.

13. "No, the uniforms didn't really fit. We just made 'em fit the best we could, you know, just for appearance sake" (Tuggle, July 8, 1985).

14. On October 13, 1934, the deputy sheriff who had been in charge of the convicts when they escaped committed suicide at the city jail, apparently because of the escape (*TD*, October 14, 1934, p. 1). Legenza, described as "a gangster-killer" and the "brains" of a tri-state gang of racketeers (*TD*, February 2, 1935, p. 1), and Mais were implicated in a series of gang-style slayings and robberies, which they apparently continued during their escape (*TD*, February 2, 1935, pp. 1, 3). Coincidentally, these two gangsters went to Philadelphia following their escape and stayed there until Legenza broke his legs in a jump to avoid capture by Philadelphia police. They then fled to New York, where they were later captured by federal agents and returned to Richmond on January 22, 1935. They were executed on February 2, 1935.

Chapter 3

1. Transcript of the Testimony in the Preliminary Hearing of the Case of the *Commonwealth of Virginia* vs. *Willie Leroy Jones*, June 24, 1983, p. 34.
2. Ibid., p. 36.
3. *Commonwealth of Virginia* vs. *Linwood Earl Briley*, December 14, 1979, January 3, 1980, January 11, 1980, and January 12, 1980, Vol. II, p. 1150.
4. Ibid., Vol. I, 74.
5. Ibid., Vol. II, 857.
6. Ibid., Vol. II, 1181.
7. This charge might have been in Linwood Briley's mind when he explained during his September 29, 1984, press conference that when he was a young boy scout, he used to catch pigeons in the alley and to catch rabbits that had escaped form a neighbor's cage to return them to him.
8. Linwood Briley tried to counter the implication that their choice of pets suggested any depravity. He noted that his snake was only twelve or thirteen inches long at the time, that he had no piranha, only two Oscar fish, a "little tarantula spider" that was harmless, and two Doberman pinschers that were just puppies when he was arrested (*TD*, September 30, 1984, p. 4).
9. The Barton Avenue murders are the ones that most frequently find their way into inmate accounts of the Brileys' crimes.
10. Sgt. Norman Harding, presently supervisor of Sex Crimes and Homicide Investigations for the City of Richmond, first met Linwood Briley when he investigated this crime in 1970. He was

in charge of the investigation of the string of homicides in which Linwood was implicated in 1979, and was one of the arresting officers. He recalls the case as one of the most involved of his career (he has been with the Richmond Police since 1962).

11. This statement, often quoted to show his cavalier reaction to the taking of a life, was presented in a different tone to Reverend Brown; "[Linwood] overheard someone say that the autopsy revealed that she would have died anyway because she had a bad heart, so he wonders whether or not she died from the gunshot wound or died from the shock."

12. Details of the following five crimes in which the Brileys were implicated were provided by Sgt. Harding (interview, June 5, 1985) and/or the Richmond Newspapers (see *NL*, July 6, 1984, p. 14; *NL*, October 11, 1984, p. 6; and *NL*, October 15, 1984, p. 10, for a few of the many references to these cases in the Richmond papers). The cases were not prosecuted because the Brileys had already been sentenced to death: "You can't burn a guy but one time," Commonwealth Attorney Aubrey Davis explained (*NL*, July 6, 1984, p. 14).

13. *Commonwealth of Virginia* vs. *Linwood Earl Briley*, February 19–February 22, 1980, p. 470.

14. *Commonwealth of Virginia* vs. *Linwood Earl Briley*, December 14, 1979, January 3, 1980, January 11, 1980, and January 12, 1980, Vol. II, p. 733.

15. Ibid., p. 856.

16. *Commonwealth of Virginia* vs. *James Dyral Briley*, January 23-25, 1980, Vol. II, p. 71.

17. September 3, 1979, is in the Department of Corrections records; newspaper accounts list his parole date as August 31, 1979 and August 21, 1979; and testimony at his trial indicates he was released on August 31, 1979.

18. Ibid., Vol. III, p. 128.

19. Upon his arrest in Philadelphia, Linwood Briley reportedly told Agent Michael Carbonell that he had been framed because he was Black (interview, June 25, 1985).

20. An earlier wedding of Death Row inmate Earl Clanton took place at Mecklenburg in 1984.

Chapter 4

1. Accounts suggest that the Brileys had a great deal more money. The *TD* for May 26, 1985, reported that they had several hundred

dollars [p. A-2], and Stockton alleged that before the escape he
held a bankroll that could have been as much as $3000 for James
Briley while he played ball [*Pilot*, September 16, 1984, p. C-11].

2. Two hours before he left home for Linwood Briley's execution,
Reverend Brown received a call from a man who asked him to
get him through to someone who could stop the execution. He
said, "I know Briley is innocent and I can prove it."

Chapter 5

1. Tuggle thinks he would have made it to Canada if he had not
had to spend money on Jones. When I asked if he, therefore,
bore any resentment toward Jones, he explained that it wasn't
Jones's fault that he had no money, and he could understand his
desire to be free too (July 8, 1985).

2. The amazing fact that Tuggle had not been detected in this truck
which they had stolen over a week earlier is partly explained by
the fact that, according to one FBI agent, the stolen vehicle had
been variously described by its owner and his son. One description had noted that the truck was black; it was blue, but had
been custom painted.

3. A *TD* article (May 26, 1985) indicates that Skip visited the Brileys
over a period of days, but Agent Carbonell says the first and only
day he went to the garage was the afternoon of the arrest.

Chapter 6

1. See Stephen B. Oates, *The Fires of Jubilee* (New York: New American Library, 1975), 117, 164-65.

2. Rule 2 under "Specific Duties" in the guide for control room
guards, states "Never leave the Control Room unless properly
relieved by your building supervisor" (appended to "An Evaluation of Training in the Virginia Department of Corrections and
the Mecklenburg Correctional Center").

3. The suit outlined thirteen charges of cruelty suffered by inmates
and contended that conditions at Mecklenburg were "beneath
standards of human decency" ("Report of the Mecklenburg Correctional Center Study Committee," p. 150). As a result of the
out-of-court settlement of this lawsuit prisoners were allowed,
among other things, more showers, more time for exercise,

increased recreational time, increased access to the law library, improved medical and psychiatric care, and additional job and educational programs, and certain limitations were placed upon the use of physical restraints.

4. "An Evaluation of Training in the Virginia Department of Corrections and the Mecklenburg Correctional Center," [Summer 1984], p. 10.

5. The figures in the following section are based on newspaper and television reports as well as on the Report of the Mecklenburg Correctional Center Study Committee, November 7, 1984. Where discrepancies appeared in the various sources, I have treated the Report of the Mecklenburg Correctional Center Study Committee as the authoritative source.

6. "Fiscal Year Escape Summary," prepared by the Department of Corrections, July 8, 1985. In 1974 population figures included misdemeanants, whereas in other years cited they include only felons. In 1974 the overall population was 5,886; the felon only population was 5,306.

7. C Building and M Building have long been notorious as the toughest buildings in the two penitentiaries. Both buildings have extensive security and inmates are locked in their cells at all times except for showers and occasional recreation. The buildings are used to house men who require protective custody and those who are being punished for infractions. Men confined to isolation are allowed no TVs or radios and no books other than the Bible. Others are not allowed TVs, but they can listen to radios and read books of their choice. Furthermore, one prisoner at the State Penitentiary told me, "the beds [in C-Cell] are as hard as the floor" (November 26, 1984). As much as inmates always dreaded confinement in these two buildings, before the changes, they all agreed Mecklenburg was the worst prison to be in.

Chapter 7

1. June Purcell Guild, *Black Laws of Virginia: A Summary of the Legislative Acts of Virginia Concerning Negroes from Earliest Times to the Present* (New York: Negro Universities Press, 1969; reprinted from 1936 Whittet and Shepperson edition), p. 154; hereafter cited in text.

2. Philip J. Schwarz, "So Many Enemies: Slaves and Crime in Virginia," unpublished manuscript, p. 3.

3. Schwarz, p. 106; George M. Stroud, *A Sketch of the Laws Relating*

to Slavery in the Several States of the United States of America (Philadelphia, 1856; cited in Schwarz, p. 48; Schwarz, p. 105.

4. Raymond Fosdick, *American Police System* (1920; rpt. Montclair, N. J.: Patterson Smith Reprint Series, 1972), 45.

5. While a couple of instances of people having been executed in Virginia localities for killing Blacks have been documented in the 18th century (and were called to my attention by Philip Schwarz), I have been unable, after exhaustive searching, to find any evidence in contemporary times to contradict Attorney J. Lloyd Snook's accusations that James Briley was the first person executed by the State of Virginia for killing a Black victim (see *NL*, September 7, 1985, p. 11).

6. William J. Bowers, *Legal Homicide: Death as Punishment in America, 1864-1962* (Boston: Northeastern Univ. Press, 1984), pp. 514-19. The Supreme Court's *Furman* vs. *Georgia* ruling, June 29, 1972, found capital punishment to be "rare, arbitrary, and discriminatory" in its application and effectively stopped executions in this country for several years.

7. Statistics furnished by the Community Services Office, City of Richmond, January 2, 1986, January 3, 1986, and January 6, 1986. Two additional people were killed in Richmond during 1985, but their deaths were ruled justifiable homicides. One of those counted among the 1985 tally died in a fire in 1984 but was not declared a homicide until 1985; another was shot in 1984 but did not die until 1985.

8. *Virginia Law Review*, 1972; cited in Bowers, p. 71.

9. Bowers, p. 159.

10. Figures compiled by the Southern Coalition on Jails and Prisons and reported in the *NL*, June 27, 1985, p. 4; see also *Time*, December 24, 1984, pp. 18, 20.

11. Versions appear in Newman White, *American Negro Folk-songs* (Hatboro, Penn: Folklore Associates, 1965), and the WPA manuscripts.

12. Traditional blues line; see Davie Evans, *Big Road Blues* (Berkeley: Univ. of California Press, 1982), p. 34.

13. *Jet*, May 13, 1985, p. 40.

14. An 1845 Virginia resolution attacking federal interference with slavery notes, "For many years after the adoption of the Constitution, the guaranty of the right to recapture fugitive slaves was held *sacred* by the people of the North" and goes on to attack the North for providing trials for such slaves, thereby aiming "insidious blows at the institution of slavery through the forms of honest legislation" (Guild, p. 205; italics mine).

15. When I asked Sgt. Harding about this, he told me he assumes that they were not aware that they were being followed that night until they left the Barton Avenue address. When they recognized that they were being followed, they were able to elude their pursuers (interview, Richmond, June 5, 1985). The focus here on the distrust that some Blacks have of the system of justice is not intended to contradict the fact that there was a great deal of evidence to establish their guilt and that a number of people involved in the case are convinced that they were guilty.

16. Johnson asked fellow inmates, guards, counselors, and other staff at the Virginia State Penitentiary to write their reaction to the execution of Coppola. He gave me copies of 51 of the 525 responses that he said he received from a population of about 900 inmates. To a man the prisoners attacked capital punishment as cruel and racist in these responses. (There are inmates at that penitentiary who have expressed agreement with capital punishment; they may simply have been reluctant to express it in this survey.) The one guard who responded supported capital punishment, writing simply, "I believe in an eye for an eye."

17. Kathi King, operations officer at the Virginia State Penitentiary, told me that contact visits are granted to close family members—mother, father, wife, children—and that had a request been made, the son could have had a contact visit with his father (August 14, 1985).

18. At the Virginia State Penitentiary, shortly before the execution, it is traditional to put the condemned man in the front cell, which is closer to the electric chair and which allows better surveillance. The cell is completely furnished with fresh linens on the bed (King).

19. All of the clocks in the area (the cell, the hall, and the execution chamber) are synchronized with the governor's office.

20. The knees were visible because of the fact that the specially prepared outfit had the right leg of the pants split in order to facilitate the placing of electrodes on the leg. One prisoner who talked to me about how traumatic he had found his job of "dressing the dude for execution" told me he had to remove the metal buttons from the jeans and the buttons from the shirt and replace them with velcour because during a prior execution a doctor had burned himself on the buttons when he went to open the shirt and check the heart (Virginia State Penitentiary, February 18, 1985).

21. The last Black executed in Virginia and the last person executed for 20½ years before Copolla was Carroll L. Garland, who was executed on March 2, 1962.

1. Grier and Cobbs, *Black Rage*, 55.
2. "Some Varieties of Heroes in America," *Journal of the Folklore Institute*, 3 (1967), 342.
3. "The Bad Man Be Stylin' for Days," in *Values in Conflict: Blacks and the American Ambivalence Toward Violence*, ed. Charles A. Frye (Washington, D.C.: University Press of America, 1980), pp. 3-4.
4. "Raps" are very popular forms in which the "rapper" recites rhythmical verses in rhyming couplets, frequently accompanied by music, popularly by "scratching," where the DJ manipulates the turntable as the record is played to produce new rhythms. Contemporary raps are considered by some to be a product of the hip-hop culture, a street culture where guys on street corners had rap contests.

Index

Long Gone